A Book of Po

"Things You Wanted To Say"

by Maria Victoria Hughes

BALBOA.
PRESS

A DIVISION OF HAY HOUSE

Balboa Press books may be ordered through booksellers or by contacting:

Balboa Press
A Division of Hay House
1663 Liberty Drive
Bloomington, IN 47403
www.balboapress.com
1 (877) 407-4847

Because of the dynamic nature of the Internet, any web addresses or links contained in this book may have changed since publication and may no longer be valid. The views expressed in this work are solely those of the author and do not necessarily reflect the views of the publisher, and the publisher hereby disclaims any responsibility for them.

The author of this book does not dispense medical advice or prescribe the use of any technique as a form of treatment for physical, emotional, or medical problems without the advice of a physician, either directly or indirectly. The intent of the author is only to offer information of a general nature to help you in your quest for emotional and spiritual well-being. In the event you use any of the information in this book for yourself, which is your constitutional right, the author and the publisher assume no responsibility for your actions.

Certain stock imagery © Thinkstock.
Any people depicted in stock imagery provided by Thinkstock are models, and such images are being used for illustrative purposes only.

ISBN: 978-1-4525-9487-3 (e)
ISBN: 978-1-4525-9486-6 (sc)
ISBN: 978-1-4525-9488-0 (hc)

Library of Congress Control Number: 2014905596

Printed in the United States of America.

Balboa Press rev. date: 11/18/2014

Table of Contents

Table of Contents

Table of Contents

Love

VOICES OF YOUTH

In the stillness of the night
I still hear your voice
It is the voice of your youth,
And as I whisper my response,
My spirit lifts.
Knowing we never change
Within me, I hear your voice,
The voice of your youth and mine.
I can feel your hands on my shoulders,
And sense the scent of sea-salt and Coppertone
As we walked along the beach.

Is joy only in youth?
Can it not spill over into our later years,
Or is it that the toil of living
Stifles our laughter.
We are not changed,
We are only living in a different time frame.
So in the stillness of the night
I can still hear your voice,
And it is the voice of your youth,
And as I whisper my response,
My spirit lifts
Knowing we never change
Within our being, we are,
Forever,
As we were,
That beautiful summer day.

DAYS OF LONG AGO

Little girls serving tea
At make-believe tea parties
Little boys in fireman hats playing fireman
Ten year olds screeching with delight –
Playing "whip" on roller skates...

Children's laughter on sleds coming down icy hills..
Teenagers meeting in the ice cream parlor...
Young men and women falling in love,
Brides in white,
Bashful grooms,
Days of You and Me...

SHARE YOUR HEART WITH ME

Speak to me in tender tones,
Walk with me on golden beaches,
Sail with me on emerald seas,
Glide with me on silver ice,
Dance with me on pink clouds,
Dream with me on balmy, summer nights.
Share your heart with me,
I have already given you all of mine.

LOVE IS

Love is all around
Love is everything and sometimes - nothing.
You hold the key to accepting love.
Love is a blind child hugging and kissing his black teacher.
Love is a deaf child smiling
At a picture of a band playing crescendo.
Love is you – As you hold my hand.
Love is giving and love is receiving
Love is the voice of the soul.

COMPLETING THE CIRCLE

I knew you once in another life.
I remember your warmth, and
The comfort I found in your arms.
A great sadness comes over me
When I remember what it felt like
To be without the security of your presence.

Now you are here in my life once again.
We have been blessed for we are together again,
To complete the circle of love that was broken so long ago.

We have searched for each other through the centuries,
And have felt the loss in each new lifetime,
Bracing ourselves from the pain by never loving again.

Now we are together,
And once more our hearts are entwined,
In a never-ending circle,
As we soar toward unknown and unseen skies.
Locked together in this time.

Let us treat this love carefully and with great tenderness.
Let us treasure it as we treasure our very souls.

We have been brought together to complete
What began so long ago.
The search is over,
The treasure of love re-discovered,
Now we are one.

MY LOVE OF YESTERDAY

Yesterday, I saw you again, after such a long time.
Today, I asked myself, "Why did I leave you long ago?"
Yesterday, we laughed, talked and
Made believe I never hurt you.
But it was there in your every unspoken word.
It was there even as you spoke
And in every glance away.
Now, I know that I should have stayed.
Today, you were too kind.
That hurt me as much as I hurt you long ago.
One never really forgives does one?
Hurt can be covered up, not thought of for years,

Then...
A familiar scent, a special season of the year,
A meeting after so long, and all the pain returns.
Did I tell you today that I regret so much?
Strange, you remembered almost everything I ever said.
I had forgotten.
The one who inflicts pain does not remember,
The stricken one remembers.
Now, the scales are balanced.
You are, unreachable, untouchable, unforgiving.
I extended my hand and gave you a glimpse of my heart and regret.
You took my hand, and in that gesture, broke my heart.
Maybe I'll see you again in another time.
And we will be together in perfect harmony and love.
Having learned what we lost,
You, early in life – me , later on.

I HAVE ALWAYS LOVED YOU

I thought I wasn't capable of love
I felt something was lacking within me,
Something I was born without.

And yet, there were times,
I found myself drifting back to the
Sun drenched hills of Spain,

Holding your hand as you spoke of your love.
Greeting you each morning with love and joy,

And one day saying goodbye in a cold train station.
I have lived so long alone,
Thinking I was incapable of love,
But you came to me in a dream,
And spoke to me of love and hope,
And my heart remembered.
I once had loved and had been loved.
I still love – you.

LET TONIGHT BE FOREVER

Tonight for a while I own you.
Tomorrow will come
And with daybreak – heartbreak.
For in the hustle of the real world
It's no longer you and me –
But we and they and you and them.
Come back to me.
Let me feel again and live again
If only in the darkness.

FIRE OF LOVE

Our love was like a fire burning brightly
With colors of orange and gold
The flames continued growing as our love grew
They seemed to reach the sky
And fill the universe.
And slowly, ever so slowly
The bright flames
Began to dim and grow smaller
Like a beautiful bonfire as it slowly burns down,
It began to lose its warmth and strength
Being fed less and less the fire of love.
As the flame and fire of love
Burnt lower and lower,
One could see the steel foundation
that would not burn away,
It was blackened and curled,
Still existing.
How like lost love this is.
After the fire has burnt itself out,
the damaged foundation of the memory remains.
One day, when we are stronger,
We can discard that steel foundation.
Then we can seek and find a love that does not need
To have it's fires fed, but exists forever
Because it's true, built on a foundation
Of mutual trust and understanding.

MYSELF

I have never loved before,
And I find it
So difficult
To give you, myself,
But myself is nothing without you.

A GLIMPSE OF SPIRIT

I looked into your eyes today,
And saw your soul.
The beauty exposed there
Took my breath away.
I felt our spirits touch,
And a bond so strong form between us
That I knew,
Nothing in this man-made world could break.

A silver, mystical cord
So strong that it will extend through time
And will stay intact, without change
As beautiful and as perfect
As that time in space when it was forged
I looked into your eyes today,
And saw that you too understood.

We have a love that has surpassed time
And will continue through eternity and beyond.

THE WONDER OF YOU

The wonder of you.
The beauty of your touch
The clarity in your eyes
Your belief in me
Your kindness and shyness,
The warmth of your closeness,
The security of your nearness,
The confusion in your face
When you don't understand what I am saying –
These are the things that I will never forget.

A LOVER'S QUESTIONS

Did I hear you say you love me?
How can that be,
When you say you love someone else too?
Once in a lifetime, the Gods of Love
Allow two souls to meet again,
Shall we toss this moment away
For duty, for commitment?
Love is a magical gift
That only comes to us when we are ready to receive it.
Refusing the gift, you must search in many lifetimes to be offered it again.
So, if you love me , accept the gift.
Let this lifetime be the one we share,
For if we lose this moment and turn away from each other,
How many more lifetimes will we have to live until we meet and love again.

THE CHAIRMAN OF THE BOARD

He was my youth, my hope,
My love, my joy,
A man who proved you can succeed
Despite where you come from or who you are.
We all know of times we may have "bit off more than we could chew"
Encouraged by him, we held on, and did it our way, as he did,
Small, tall, American, foreign, we knew we would succeed.
He gave us strength and courage to keep on going against all odds.
Right or wrong,, rich or poor, he spoke to us and for us.
He laughed, he cried, he believed in brotherhood,
He pulled us through, and was a symbol, letting us know,
We can do it - "Our" way.
God's blessing, a warrior, a troubadour, fresh, kind, wild, soft
Our gift...Frank

MY ROMAN SOLDIER

Sitting in he glow of your love,
I find my mind has left my body
As I fly back through time and space
Going to a day when I knew you so long ago.
You were my Roman soldier, I, your Grecian bride.
Standing on a windy hill we parted.
You departed for battle promising to return.
I knew that was not to be.

You never returned.
And now you are here again,
Yet, we are separated again, by more than time,
We live different lives, with different people.
Yet, somehow we know that once we were together,
And will be once again, but not in this lifetime.
This unspoken love that we have for each other
Has continued through the centuries and has never ceased.
We live our daily lives now, knowing
One day we will once again be re-united.
Where or when doesn't matter,
For our heart and soul prints are still etched
In time on that windy hill in Rome.
Dear one I will wait until that day.

THE GIFT OF LOVE

I have never loved before,
And I find it so difficult to
Give you – Myself.
But Myself is nothing without you.

MY OWN MARCELLO MASTROIANNI

He was my solace in the storm that was my life.
My shore of safety in the troubled seas of my days.
I was a child,
I didn't understand
The loneliness and terror that encompassed me.
I was a child,
Yet I did understand
That wherever he was,
I was safe.

A child of a broken marriage
Like a boat without a mooring,
I lived my life like a buoy,
Bouncing up and down on the waves of my days.

During that journey
He became my anchor,
Somehow he helped me to safely reach shore.
Even now, I feel the love,
Kindness and understanding he gave me
And always will,
I love you Uncle Jim,
My own Marcello Mastroianni

ONCE SOMEONE LOVED ME

Once someone loved me.
I didn't realize then what it meant.
A man so strong, so joyful and kind,

To me, he was very big,
My small hand almost lost in his.
He gave me a sense that I would always be safe.
As he lifted me high above the ground,
Held by his strong hands, I knew no fear.

Once someone loved me.
And when he left, I was lost.
I searched for him in every face I encountered,
And failed to find him.
For he had gone to a place I could not enter.
Then one day I turned within,
And I found what I thought was lost,
Still lived in my heart..

People go away,
Days become dark and gray.
It's then that I remember
That in that place where memories live,
The Sun is always shining,
Roses are always in bloom.
The child is safe and loved,
Love remains unchanged, untarnished
As bright as it was that day
When someone loved me.

I SEE YOU EVERYWHERE

I can't get away from you.
I traveled to London and saw you in every face.

In the gesture of the cab driver,
And in the young Irishman's smile.
I saw your eyes looking out at me
From the eyes of the Concierge,
I heard your laughter in Piccadilly Circus.

Bumped and jostled in the crowd.
I saw you at the Tower,
A young man holding his son's hand,
I caught a glimpse of you at Buckingham Palace,
Holding your daughter up
to watch the "Changing of the Guard."

I paused, for I felt lost and you tipped your hat
and asked if you could help.

What was this I was seeing...
Was I haunted by the memory of you.
And then it came to me,
I looked up at the steeple of St Paul's Cathedral
And knew,
I was seeing - love.
For there are no barriers,
Of time, space and place,
No words, no memories,
There is only an unforgettable love
That endures forever.

THOUGHTS OF YOU

When I'm alone with my thoughts,
I am with you again,
Seeing your smile, hearing your laugh,
Feeling your touch, sharing your wine,
Touching your face,
Cherishing the memories…
When we shared those magical moments

COME BACK TO ME

Silence touches me like a velvet glove.
Your voice brings me back to green hills and sun bleached meadows.
The times spent walking and touching silence hand in hand.
A Love so beautiful, so encompassing
Can not be experienced again
The memories I have are of another time
And they have faded in the passing of time
But deep in dreams you come to me
I cannot see your face
Yet, I plead Come back to me…..Come back to me…..
Who are you…
What is your name?
In my soul I know these things
But here, now---I can't remember.
Come back to me,
I sense you are around me
And know, I must wait until once more you return,
Whether in this time, or in another lifetime.
I promise, I shall wait.

DID YOU SAY YOU LOVE ME?

Did I hear you say you loved me?
How can that be, when you say you love someone else too?
And you don't know what to do.
How can that be ?
Once in a lifetime, the Gods of Love allow two souls to meet again,
Shall we toss this moment away
For duty, for commitment?
Love is a magical gift
That only comes to us when we are ready to receive it.
Refusing the gift, you must search for many lifetimes to be offered it again.
So, if you love me,
Accept the gift.
Let this lifetime be the one we share,
For if we lose this moment and turn away from each other,
How many more lifetimes will we have to live
Until we meet and love again.

SHIFTING SANDS

Standing by the shore,
Watching the sand slowly drift away,
My thoughts go back to the day we met.
We shared a love
Like the rush of ocean waves,
Vibrant, wild and beautiful in its intensity.
Like the wave
It didn't last.
It drifted away slowly like the sand,
Leaving no trace - just a memory
Of what might have been.

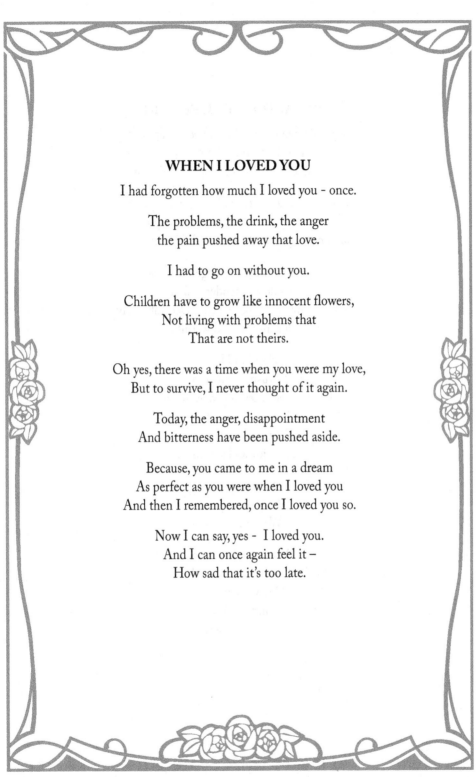

WHEN I LOVED YOU

I had forgotten how much I loved you - once.

The problems, the drink, the anger
the pain pushed away that love.

I had to go on without you.

Children have to grow like innocent flowers,
Not living with problems that
That are not theirs.

Oh yes, there was a time when you were my love,
But to survive, I never thought of it again.

Today, the anger, disappointment
And bitterness have been pushed aside.

Because, you came to me in a dream
As perfect as you were when I loved you
And then I remembered, once I loved you so.

Now I can say, yes - I loved you.
And I can once again feel it –
How sad that it's too late.

FORWARD TO THE FUTURE

Today the winter wind whipped me around,
And pushed me back to the past.
I remembered wintry days spent with you.

Racing down the street, with bright, red cheeks,
My coat blown open, hardly warming me.
But, knowing I would see you, I felt nothing.

Warmed by the knowledge that soon
Your smile and tender embrace
Would fill my heart and the cold December day
With sunshine and warmth.

Hand in Hand
We rushed down the
Frosty streets, certain we were going
Forward to a future
Where everyday was
Full of joy and sunshine.

We were young.
We were hopeful.
We were wrong.

We married - others,
And now all that lies ahead
Are wintry days
Windy and cold
Like our love.

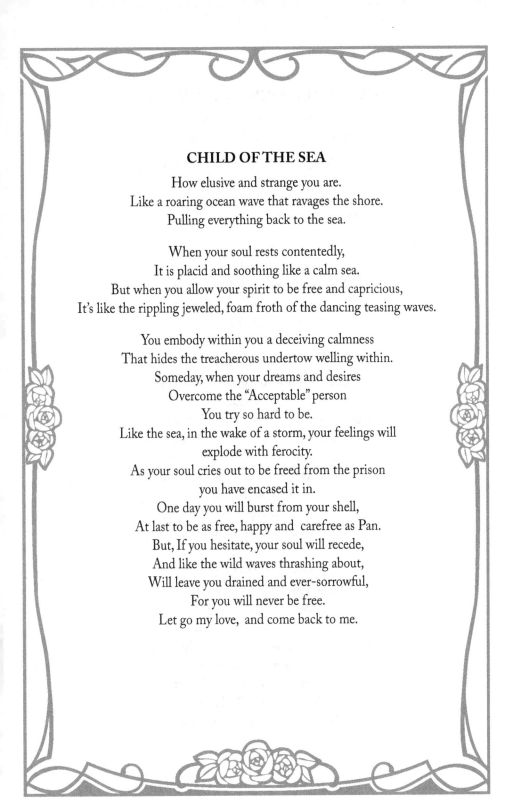

CHILD OF THE SEA

How elusive and strange you are.
Like a roaring ocean wave that ravages the shore.
Pulling everything back to the sea.

When your soul rests contentedly,
It is placid and soothing like a calm sea.
But when you allow your spirit to be free and capricious,
It's like the rippling jeweled, foam froth of the dancing teasing waves.

You embody within you a deceiving calmness
That hides the treacherous undertow welling within.
Someday, when your dreams and desires
Overcome the "Acceptable" person
You try so hard to be.
Like the sea, in the wake of a storm, your feelings will
explode with ferocity.
As your soul cries out to be freed from the prison
you have encased it in.
One day you will burst from your shell,
At last to be as free, happy and carefree as Pan.
But, If you hesitate, your soul will recede,
And like the wild waves thrashing about,
Will leave you drained and ever-sorrowful,
For you will never be free.
Let go my love, and come back to me.

LOVE IS LIKE A WAVE IN THE OCEAN

Standing by the shore,
Watching the sand slowly wash away,

My thoughts go back to the day we met.
We shared a love
Like the rush of ocean waves,
Vibrant, wild and beautiful in its intensity.

Like the wave
It didn't last.
It drifted away slowly like the sand,
Leaving no trace - just a memory
Of what might have been.

MY DREAM

Yesterday I was young and full of hope
But fearful.
Today I am no longer young, and I have no fear.
But…I live with the knowledge
That I did not accomplish the things I dreamed about.
Because I didn't have the courage to pursue them.
I followed the rules,
Did the Right Thing
And lost my dream.

FORBIDDEN LOVE

Our eyes dance when we meet
We smile at each other
From deep within our being.
As you held me closely, on that bright Sunday,
The world disappeared.
For a moment only you and I existed
Then - you walked away
And it was raining in New York.

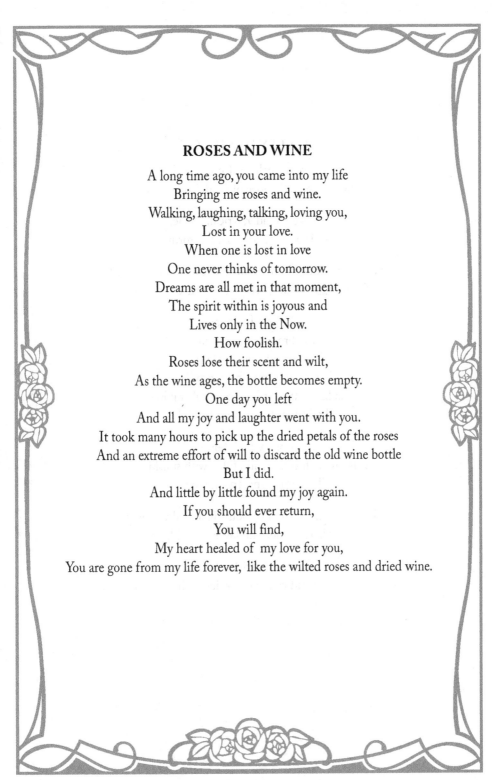

ROSES AND WINE

A long time ago, you came into my life
Bringing me roses and wine.
Walking, laughing, talking, loving you,
Lost in your love.
When one is lost in love
One never thinks of tomorrow.
Dreams are all met in that moment,
The spirit within is joyous and
Lives only in the Now.
How foolish.
Roses lose their scent and wilt,
As the wine ages, the bottle becomes empty.
One day you left
And all my joy and laughter went with you.
It took many hours to pick up the dried petals of the roses
And an extreme effort of will to discard the old wine bottle
But I did.
And little by little found my joy again.
If you should ever return,
You will find,
My heart healed of my love for you,
You are gone from my life forever, like the wilted roses and dried wine.

LONELY IRISH BOY

Today is your birthday, Lonely Irish Boy
Torn between the love of God, Love of me.

You were tender, lyrical, poetic,
Full of laughter and tears, and torment.

One who has longed for a mother's love, so long denied.
Spurning the truth, because it hurts too much.

Lonely Irish boy,
You brought me sunshine,
You brought me tenderness,
You brought me feelings of love
You brought me three beautiful children
And I loved you so, and still do.

Lonely Irish boy,
It is my wish you are still filled with sunshine,
Tenderness, poetry and love.

There are three who love you still and always will.
There is one, who loves you still.

Lonely Irish boy,
How sad you never believed that.

When Love Is Gone

LOVE

Love is a strange emotion.
It's like an exquisite jewel that
Sparkles and shines, yet is hard to the touch.
Yes, love is like that.
It's beautiful and should be lasting.
Gives joy and sometimes pain.
Like a jewel you can protect and polish it,
But it is always a thing apart.
A thing alone.
It never really belongs to you.
Like the jewel, it must be carefully taken care of,
It must be treasured and never neglected or misplaced.
For then it can be lost,
And never found again.
And if someone takes it from you,
They will never give it back.

UNDYING LOVE?

You swear your undying love,
And then don't speak to me for weeks.
I thought you were my champion,
But you are a facade like those used on Hollywood sets.
I know this,
And still cannot understand why I care,
Or why I am so angry at myself.

THE END OF THE STORY

I sit here alone now.
I, who a few years ago was assailed
With loud voices, children's laughter, kisses and hugs,
Dirty dishes, pots filled with left-overs,
And the wondrous glow of being a mother and wife.

They're grown now, each off in their own direction.
And so are you.
I won't ever really lose them, I'll just slowly keep letting go.
While moments like this tear me apart
With yearning for the sound
Of bouncing steps and cheerful voices,
I know they are on their own journey.
But do you know you've lost me ?
It seems we were tightly held together
By the cords of mother and fatherhood, and fulfilled our duty.
We were ideal parents, never ideal lovers or friends.
You took my joy away with angry words,
Beseeching phrases, constant criticism.
Every worry of mine, you shrugged off,
Every lovely thought, you never sought or listened to.
They grew. We didn't.
We go now in different directions.
Never to meet again at the crossroads of joy and love.
We never really knew each other.
It comes to two sentences.
I am I, You are You,
IT'S OVER.

LOVE –STORMY LIKE THE OCEAN

Standing by the shore,
Watching the sand slowly wash away,

My thoughts go back to the day we met.
We shared a love
Like the rush of ocean waves,
Vibrant, wild and beautiful in its intensity.
Like the wave
It didn't last.

It drifted away slowly like the sand,
Leaving no trace - just a memory
Of what might have been.

I AM A CHILD

Hold me close
One last time.
Forgive my cruelty and anger.
Hold the child within me.
Don't let me go.
The child is lost, lonely and frightened.
The adult is
Composed and cool,
Yet within, lost, lonely and frightened.
The child can accept your love.
The adult cannot.
You don't understand
And you walk away.
The child understands.
The adult cries.

CRUSHED ROSES

Did I tell you my heart was broken?
Did you know that you crushed the rose within my heart
The one that held all my love for you.
Did you hear me speak softly and gently to you
Asking you to understand…to believe…to stay…to love.
Did you know that when words are bitter and angry
They destroy the garden of love.
That garden of love in one's heart.
It's over now.
But after the rain the sun will come out again.
And plant a garden of roses in my heart.
Roses that will bloom again
More sweet smelling and beautiful than ever before.
For there is someone who will cherish and care for them forever.
So, when morning comes, and the sun shines brightly,
I will rise with the sun and find my joy and peace restored.
For, the roses in the garden of my heart will
bloom again for someone new.

WHAT DO I WANT

I want to walk on beaches
I want to speak to someone
About this loneliness and fear within.
I want to be young and carefree again,
Was I ever?
I want my mother to be young again.
I want the days to be long, and the nights short.
I want to wear high, high heels
and a white bathing suit at the beach
I want to stand on a stage and be applauded.
I want the world to love me.
Most of all, I want someone to listen.

FORBIDDEN LOVE

Our eyes dance when we meet
We smile at each other from deep
Within our being.
Today you held me,
And the world disappeared.
For a moment only you and I existed
Then you walked away
And it rained again in New York.

YOU'VE WALKED OUT AGAIN

Why is it that now memories of you seem so happy?
When you were here, I was safe, I was secure.
I belonged to someone once – it was you.

And although we were not together anymore,
You were still there.
And I could still complain about you.
Still criticize you, still anger you,
Still depend on you.

Was the burden too great?
I guess I lived in a dream world,
Believing, that without words,
You too, thought of me.

I was wrong.
You truly left long ago
Vowing never to return,
And now you can't.
I'm really angry with you.

FALSE LOVER

Two Martini's turn you into a lover,
Three Martini's a poet, and sage,
With four Martini's you become DaVinci.

Do you really think I don't know you?
I recognize you in every man who is in love
But by his self-professed morality – is in prison.
A prison of his own making, yet a prison nonetheless.

Can you imagine how you would feel if you freed your spirit.
This does not mean leaving or changing what you now love,
It means just "being" you.

Look deep inside – feel that secret place stir.
Know what it feels like to giggle like a child,
Make eyes at someone, with the eyes you had as a fourth-grader
Give your love freely with all your strength,
The way you hugged your teddy bear,
With all your strength and all your love.

When you do, those you do love will know it,
And, you are the one, who will reap the most benefits,
For you will finally have loved someone more than you love you.

ALWAYS ALONE

All my life I have been searching
For something to fill the void – within me.
That never seemed to be closed. What was it that I missed?
Did it start with not having a mother's love..
Or the presence of a father? I think it was there the day I was born.
I remember the feeling as a child,
Always, just a little bit sad.
The smile, the laugh, the charm, the talent
A cover-up to fool the world. A world that only saw the smiling,
Laughing, charming, happy me. Not the lonely, lost me.
I too did not want the world to see. So I did the things all good children do.
I behaved correctly like all good girls do.
I grew and matured outwardly like all good young ladies do.
And the void became a gap and widened and cried, strained and
begged to be filled.
I, who for so many years – could ignore the void,
Looked into my suffering, loneliness and said—Why Not!
Why shouldn't I be fulfilled? I need…I want…I desire.
I let the voice come out from deep within my being
And finally listened to its whimpering. and tried to soothe it.
I learned it couldn't be soothed by me alone. It needed somebody else.
It needed the special glow that comes when your hear,
You're lovely, I need you…Without You I cannot function.
So Now, I will listen, and to try to capture the excitement,
And yet, always wonder, why, why, did I wait so long?
Why did I suppress the voice? Why didn't I try to help me – yesterday!

MY ILLUSION

How your cowardice has disappointed me.
I thought of you as my Champion
My Knight.

But you were only acting a part.
The pursuing male
Who chases and pleads until he wins.

Although you can never win me.
You try.
I laugh.
Two egos are appeased.
And so we live our lie.

MOMENTS IN TIME

My heart was so full of you,
It was brimming over with feeling…
Wouldn't it be wonderful
If we could live in those moments forever.

But the world intrudes,
And we change,
Feeling that we must march to the
Beat of the human drummer,
And we lose so much.

The child-like faith in another person,
The love given and carelessly tossed aside,
The pain and tears that bring no ease.

The body aches and the world grieves,
Not for the lost love
But for the loss of belief.

ONCE, LONG AGO

They tell me, roses are red, violets are blue
But, you don't remember the beauty of the roses
Nor the scent of the violets
I do.
The velvet feel of the petals melted my heart,
And the scent of the violets
Lifted me to a place I will never enter again.
I remember.
Now I have only the brown, crushed petals of the roses
And a vague, lingering stale scent of the violets,
They lay, old, discarded and dead...
Like our love.

THE SEASON OF LOVE

The wind was gently blowing,
Sweet and warm it caressed my cheek.
The sun was bright and brazen,
And my world took on a golden glow.

I was with you, and my heart was dancing,
Like a wayward leaf in autumn,
Lost in a season of love, laughter, promises and joy.

I forgot.
The seasons change quickly,
The wind grows rough and bitter.
The sun becomes weak and rarely shines,
The leaves of autumn, once dancing are tossed and thrown helter-skelter,
And the world takes on a grey hue.
You've gone,
My winter has begun.

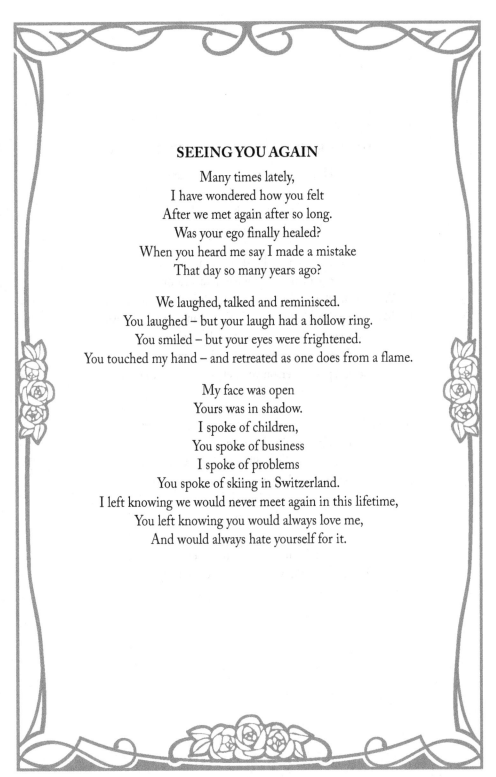

SEEING YOU AGAIN

Many times lately,
I have wondered how you felt
After we met again after so long.
Was your ego finally healed?
When you heard me say I made a mistake
That day so many years ago?

We laughed, talked and reminisced.
You laughed – but your laugh had a hollow ring.
You smiled – but your eyes were frightened.
You touched my hand – and retreated as one does from a flame.

My face was open
Yours was in shadow.
I spoke of children,
You spoke of business
I spoke of problems
You spoke of skiing in Switzerland.
I left knowing we would never meet again in this lifetime,
You left knowing you would always love me,
And would always hate yourself for it.

THE FREE SPIRIT A CHILD OF THE SEA

How elusive and strange you are.
Like a roaring ocean wave that ravages the shore
Pulling everything back to the sea.
This is how you live your life.

When your soul rests in contentment,
It is placid and withdrawn like a calm sea.
When you allow your true self to be loose and capricious
It's like the rippling, wild, foam froth of dancing, teasing waves.
A deceiving calmness and treacherous undertow
When your dreams and desires overcome
The acceptable person you believe yourself to be...
Then...

You explode with ferocity as your inner being cries out to be freed
From the self-contained person you let the world see.
Bursting from the shell you encase yourself in,
You are free, happy and as carefree as pan.
Then...
You recede
Like the wild, dangerous waves,
Leaving you drained, ashamed and ever-sorrowful
Because you know you will never be truly free.

Children & Family

YESTERDAY, WHEN THEY WERE HOME

One day I turned around and they were gone.
Rooms that once trembled with laughter, talking and crying,
Lost sneakers and forgotten lunches
Now echo with silence.
Once there were three.
One so blonde and strong.
Two so dark, different – yet so much alike.
I pause,
And ask in vain
Let me have one more moment of Mothering.
Push back the years
Let me once more kiss chubby hands,
And smell the baby softness of them.
How is it that this day came?
I should have noticed it sneaking into my world.
They tell me this is the thing called
Life
And although I know this is true..
I still ask and wish
For one more moment to mother my babies.

THE MAGIC OF A CHILDREN

Joy is of the moment
The soft touch of a baby's cheek
As it rests on yours.
How keen the hearing becomes,
When the beautiful child says,
"Nana, Can I tell you something?"
Watching the 3 yr. old little boy
Swing his trusty sword freeing the Princess
Leaning over the princess, lisping,
"Love's true kiss will wake her up."
I hold him close and he squirms,
Because hugging is not a "boy thing."
Watching the baby giggle as
The older sister and brother make funny faces.
Watching the older sister, who having started school
has learned how to…"Worry."
Why can't we still have the magic of childhood?

MY SON

Torn jeans
Unlaced sneakers
Worn out baseball glove
A graduation tassel hanging from a shelf,
Toss in a plaid shirt and a brilliant smile,
Stir with love, you have,
My Son.

MY DAUGHTER
(for Cathy)

She is magical and mystical.
She is many things in varying spaces of time.
A child, a mystic, an actress, an athlete, a leader.
She is in turn,
Joyful,
Playful,
Wistful
And aloof.

Around her a sense of mystery abides.
Like the Merlin of old,
She can change form into anything she wants to be.

When I held her in my arms,
She cuddled, then struggled to get free.
I watched her take her first steps,
And at step three - she ran off.
I remember her holding her Dr. Seuss books on her lap,
Then listened with amazement
As she recited every page - from memory.
I saw her whispering in her dog's ear,
While tears streamed down her face,
And I know the dog understood!

If she should cry,
Her tears burn like fire
And come not from her eyes - but from her very soul.
And yet, when she laughs and dances merrily about,
She's like the Pied Piper; we all follow in joy.
She is Christmas, Halloween
And Guy Fawkes Day all in one.
She is my daughter
And I love her.

MY DAUGHTERS

They danced into my life
And my joy at their presence is unexplainable.
Strong, vital, beautiful women.
Yet, to me..
Little girls I hold in my arms,
Only in my mind now..
Their delightful impishness,
Their beliefs and strong convictions, their truths,
Their contributions to this world,
This is the essence of them.
Dear God, I am grateful and honored they are in my life.
These are the words of a Mother,
Words of a Woman,
With Respect
For other Women.

MEMORIES OF BRIAN

There was a little boy on my flight who looked so much like you Brian.
A big, smiling, yet serious boy of eight or nine or so,
Who struggled to be contained in his seat,
And I thought of you – Brian.
When he said, "Mommy, Mommy, look at the mountains!"
My heart flew to him,
As it does to you – Brian.
So young, so untouched by the years,
As you once were – Brian.
So, I smiled and envied the mother,
Wishing she were me and he were you – Brian!.

I HARDLY KNOW YOU MY SON

How is it that I hardly know you my son,
Heart of my heart, blood of my blood,
With great love I set you free.

There is within me
The desire to hold you as I did
When you were a small child,
A desire that cannot be.

Go on to your life's journey,
making your own way,
Holding and kissing your children

Hold them tightly, kiss them mightily,
For the time is short that it is given to you to do so,
For, one day, you may have to say,
"My child I hardly know you."

FOOTBALL MOTHERS

From community Little League Football, on up to the Pros,
The boy who plays football is very important!
To his peers, his school, his friends and family.
At least – that is what we have been lead
To believe by our sons, fathers and husbands.

But I take this time to write not of the athletes,
But of the women who have taken care of these boys since they
have been born.
Who know them almost as well as they know themselves.
That is except when they don their football uniforms and equipment.
Then they are hardly recognizable to us.

It all starts when at age three or four they get their first football outfit.
The one with the Styrofoam shoulder pads, and plastic helmet
And father says "Wow – Great" Mom smiles and says, "Very nice."
And the years go on and the dream becomes very real to the boy in the
Joe Namath suit.
Only the name on the uniform changes

And dad says "Wow – Great." mom sighs and says, "Very nice."
The games begin – the boys batter each other.
The dads scream till they are hoarse, and later
they speak of how proud they are of their sons.

Sons, who are out there grappling, slipping, hitting, being hit...
This is bravery or the enduring of punishment?
Mom goes to the games because it is torture for her to wait at home
And torture to be there. But at least she is near her son.
She braves the cold, the wind, the rain, the snow and the comments
in the stands...
"Throw out that quarterback, Defense is awful...Offense is awful...
The running backs are too slow, on and on"

She's there because her heart is under her boy's uniform.
His slide in the mud is her heart sliding in the mud.
On every tackle she hits the ground.
But who else knows this suffering. Only another mother.
She loves him - he is her child.
She cannot stop him from battering his body into the ground.
She is the one, who has the most courage because
She does not discourage him from his dream,
So she goes along with that dream and gives him all her
love and support..
When the final whistle blows, the relief is not only felt by the winners.
But most of all by the mothers.
Win or Lose – Who Cares? As long as everyone is all right.

FOR MOM

Mom, you curled my hair, taught me songs,
And chased away the boogey man.

Mom, you held my hand at the dentist
And took the first ride with me when I got my license.
Mom, you held me close when my favorite doll broke,
When my dog died and my best friend deserted me.
You stood aside and let me grow up.

I'm all grown up now,
And yet, my heart lifts when you call me your baby.
I sit and ask myself
How many nights have you sat alone?
Who held you close?
Who dried your tears?
How very long were the days in the Nursing Home?
And yet you smiled every time you saw me,
And called me "your baby."
Now, I'm someone's "mom,"
and with all the joy I feel,
I wonder who will hold me close
Who will dry my tears, and who will hold my hand?
And I know the answer,
It will be you, from wherever you are.

THE TEENAGE YEARS OF THE FIRST DAUGHTER

I looked at your picture today, and the full force of how much
I love you hit me.
How is it that you are my daughter and I feel I know you not at all?
Your sparkling eyes dance and your smile is worth living for
And I have never felt them turned on for me.
You are a precious gift, given to me, to teach me how much
I do not know.
Your silence pierces me with its sound.
And your serenity is something I cannot ever grasp or have.
Will I ever know what goes on behind your dancing eyes?
As I watch you grow up and away,
I wonder were you ever "here?"
You are passing through my life and although I am the mother
and you the child,
I feel that there is so much you can teach me.
I must say, dearest daughter, you are everything I cannot be.
Share your dreams with me
No matter what I seem to be on the surface.
For you, I will try to understand.
Do not stand so far from me; I feel I cannot reach you.
Do you know, you will reach heights I will never know,
let me help you climb.
You will go places I will never see – let me help you see them.
You will live in a world I will not understand – but save a space for me.
I am not saying cling to me, and I promise I will not cling to you,
But let us let our spirits lean towards the same goals,
Then our minds will soar to the shores of understanding.
And you will know how much I love you,
And I will know how much you love me.

Mommy

GRADUATION

As I stand here tonight, so many memories rush in.

I see

You – at your first dance recital – out of step.

You – at your first time at bat - striking out.

You – at the cheerleading competition - losing your voice.

You - on your first day of school - Standing on the wrong line.

Time went on, and you became more sure of yourself and needed me less.

Soon - You – walked to school alone

You – rode your bike to the Mall and the Beach

You - learned to talk to the girls and boys without hitting and punching

And I realized you were growing.

The months and years flew by, and it seemed that overnight

You switched from Baby Shoes – Triple E

To Construction Boots and Sandals.

Braids were out and blow dryers were in.

Baseball and football were in, and hide and seek

Was forgotten and hidden away with the old baseball cards

and Barbie dolls.

Teachers were no longer feared –

They became friends.

My heart skipped at each new adventure and step you took into the future.

And with the glory and assurance of youth, you dashed forward.

My hope for you is..

That the future is everything you desire,

That you may never be – out of step,

Never strike out or fumble the ball.

Stay in fine voice and never get on the wrong line again

Run gladly, bravely and fearlessly into the sunshine of your future.

Where all your dreams and mine will come true.

MY SURFER CHILD
(for Carolyn)

Standing alone at the ocean's shore,
Time stands still
And I see you again
Like a photograph being enlarged.
Watching you change from age four,
Growing, Growing, Growing...
Intensely staring at the sea,
One toe poised in the sand,
Letting the tide wrap the soft sand around your ankles.
You are at one with the sand and surf.
Like a siren's call, the sea beckons to you.
You take a deep breath,
Your body alert - yet poised,
As you plunge headlong into the beautiful green foam.
At one with the sea,
You once again revert to your natural home,
And I know you're smiling.

MY SON, MY HERO
(For Brian)

Young Viking, , tender child, caring man
All these things come to mind when I think of you.
A boy, who with a smile that can heal the deepest pain.
A boy with courage, who became at seventeen,
A young man who took care of his mother and sisters,
Who cared with feelings so devastatingly strong,,
They brought tears to his eyes, that no one saw.
A boy who worked at any menial job,
And yet maintained a royal stature.
A roaring lion with a heart as big and soft as a pure cloud.
A modern day Knight – striving and fighting for right.
He took on the fight, won the battle
and claimed the prize to give to others.

THOUGHTS AT A GRADUATION

Standing there with your friends, I hardly recognize you.
Tall, confident young men,
Pretty girls with silken hair flying
Passing by me, like pages of a book.
Where is daddy's little girl now?
Is she packed away with the
Barbie Dolls and Nancy Drew books?
Where is mommy's little boy?
Is he stuffed in the back of the closet?
With the Star Trek Game and
The autographed football?
I watch their eyes, and
I hear your silent, "Oh mom – oh dad."
I wish you knew we are not
Watching you with criticism,
But with wonder, pride and love.
You all look so poised and self-assured.
But I know that inside of you is a secret, quiver of fear.
That only time, experience and maturity will ease,
Although it will not really ever go away, we who watch you know.
It will be there before every great and small event in your life.
Now, it's the exam you're not sure of.
The team, you're trying out for,
The college you weren't accepted to.
Then it will be the day you marry,
Then the day you hold your first child in your arms.
You'll go through all these tense moments,
As we did, and someday you will sit here in our place,
And watch your "once" baby walk away into adulthood.
And you too will be filled with love, wonder and pride.
And then that small secret part of you will once again, feel frightened.

THE BRIDE'S MOTHER
(for Cathy & Carolyn)

As I touch your hair, and straighten your veil,
You stand before me a beautiful, grown woman.
But as I touch your hair, I see, and feel once again
Your soft curly hair, and your tiny, clenched fists,
As they placed you in my arms, the first time I held you.

You dance around the room,
And hug me with a tight embrace,
And I see you once again - taking your first steps,
And giving me a hug,
When your arms were too tiny to go around my neck.
You stand there glowing,

And I glow with the memory of you staring with wonder
Seeing your first Christmas tree.
I see your skinned knees and witness your temper tantrums.
I can hear you say, "I'm going to tell grandma on you!"

I watch you once again, running fearlessly into the ocean,
Learning to ride a two-wheeler, then learning to drive,
And my heart still flip-flops.

I see you sitting on the floor hugging your dog
And telling him all your problems.
I see tears glistening on your face,
That you wipe with the back of a smudgy hand
Telling me you weren't invited to someone's birthday party.

I closed my eyes and mind,
Because I really didn't want to see You - growing and going away.
But you did anyway.
And I realize how rich you have made my life.
And how having you in my life has made it so full of joy and love.

You, my child, my daughter, my friend,
The new bride, taught me what love really is.
I love you.   Mommy

NOW I HAVE TIME

When you were tiny,
I wished for the time you could walk and talk.
When I could have more time for myself.
When you were three,
I longed for the day you would start school
And I would have more time for myself.
When you were ten,
I longed for the day you were in high school,
And I could drop some of the activities at your school,
And I could have more time for myself.
Now you are graduating from high school
And are going away to college.
Funny, now I long for those old days,
Now, I have the time,
To kiss your baby-fine hair,
I have the time to teach you to ride your bike,
Take you to the park, play make-believe games.
I have the time now to play catch,
I have the time to make your favorite desert…chocolate pudding.
I have the time now to sit by your bed and sing you to sleep.
I have the time now to do so much,
But now you are going,
And you have no time for those things,
And all I have is time.

YOUR WEDDING & BABY MAGIC LOTION
(For Carolyn)

The first time I watched you try on your wedding gown,
And place the crown and veil on your head,
My heart was so full of love and awe -
I could hardly speak.
Engulfed with lace and tulle, beautiful and graceful
As a fairy princess.

Then you took a step towards me,
And in my eyes you were transformed.
I saw my chubby baby, all yawns, gurgles
And Baby Magic lotion.

I was transported to the past,
Seeing you at two - birthday party crown in place.
Graciously accepting a bouquet of flowers from daddy.
Three years old, covered in flour and sugar baking "pies."
Handling a Police horse, little feet too short for any stirrup.
Five Years old - off to school without a backward glance.
Tattling on your brother and sister.
Golden days - when the sun was always shining.
Sailing through the years,
High School and Proms, College and football games at Harvard.

All your pets,
Teaching ...and falling in love with every child.
Much laughter...some tears...always love.

Today you marry,
And I watch you walk down the aisle
Smiling as you go forward to your future.
My fairy princess daughter!
Who has filled my life with joy and a special magic,
And as you glide by me, I catch the scent of Baby Magic Lotion.
Thank you God for these blessings.
With all my love, Mommy.

MY SON JUST GOT MARRIED

My son just got married!!!
The party is over, and the "Mother's Dress" has been put away.
The Thank-You cards have been received,
And the newlyweds dutifully have come over for dinner.

My son just got married!!!
And I just went into his room and tripped over his weights.
The silence was deafening.
I don't think I have ever been in an emptier room before.
All the nail holes on the wall where his pennants once hung,
Pennants that are boxed up in the garage.
His bed neatly made up – the closet empty except for
The old Superman Costume stuck on the shelf,
And the Miller's Highlight sign in the corner.

My son just got married!!!
And although I wish he and his wife only joy,
There is an emptiness within me that will never be filled.

I remember the little boy who wouldn't sign his name for his first library card.
I feel his sweaty hand in mine, on the first day of school,
tears streaming down his face.
I see him once again flying into the house so proud he made the football team.
And I shiver, thinking about the days in the stands watching him play football,
And flinching whenever someone was on the ground.
I smile with pride reliving the many awards dinners attended
And the many awards he won.
I experience once again the feeling I had when he went away to school,
And the elation I feel, every time he comes through the door.
Blue eyes and bright smile lighting up the room.

My son just got married!!!
No more bear hugs – No more sister-brother squabbling,
No mother-son talks.

My son just got married!!!
And now he belongs to another time, another person, and another place.
So I clean the room, pack up the old trophies,
And keep the small child cuddled always in my heart,
As I watch the man go further and further away.

THE DAY AFTER THE WEDDING

Did you know you left Barbie in the closet?
And the cat bowl needs to be refilled,
And there's three mis-matched sox in the drawer.

I noticed your phone was disconnected
And your teddy bear was gone.

They told me this was a time of "Adjustment,"
And I've tried to cope - God knows...

But your voice lingers in the air,
And the memory of your smile and dancing eyes
Brighten up the dark corners of the room.

I sit and see you at three, ten and sixteen..
Somehow I blinked,
And you were all grown-up.
And now you're "his wife."
Ah, but to me, you will always be "my baby."

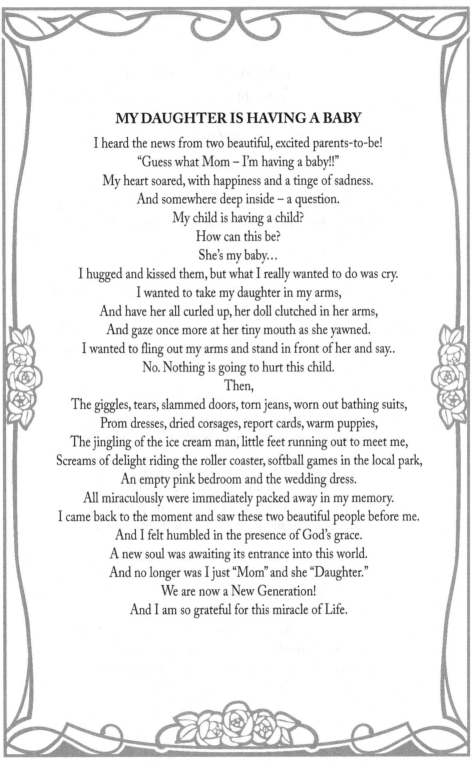

MY DAUGHTER IS HAVING A BABY

I heard the news from two beautiful, excited parents-to-be!
"Guess what Mom – I'm having a baby!!"
My heart soared, with happiness and a tinge of sadness.
And somewhere deep inside – a question.
My child is having a child?
How can this be?
She's my baby...
I hugged and kissed them, but what I really wanted to do was cry.
I wanted to take my daughter in my arms,
And have her all curled up, her doll clutched in her arms,
And gaze once more at her tiny mouth as she yawned.
I wanted to fling out my arms and stand in front of her and say..
No. Nothing is going to hurt this child.
Then,
The giggles, tears, slammed doors, torn jeans, worn out bathing suits,
Prom dresses, dried corsages, report cards, warm puppies,
The jingling of the ice cream man, little feet running out to meet me,
Screams of delight riding the roller coaster, softball games in the local park,
An empty pink bedroom and the wedding dress.
All miraculously were immediately packed away in my memory.
I came back to the moment and saw these two beautiful people before me.
And I felt humbled in the presence of God's grace.
A new soul was awaiting its entrance into this world.
And no longer was I just "Mom" and she "Daughter."
We are now a New Generation!
And I am so grateful for this miracle of Life.

WHAT DADDY WOULD HAVE SAID

He straightens his tie for the fifth time, smoothes his tuxedo jacket
looks into the mirror, touching the gray at his temples
And walks out of the Room

Almost invisible.
He passes through the group of talking, laughing, lovely women.
His daughter – The Bride is being prepared for her day, by her handmaidens.
He shakes his head and wonders, who is this beautiful stranger?

Time stands still and he remembers:
The first time he saw this daughter.
His mind takes him back to a place where he sees a beautiful, solemn child,
Who, when she giggled turned his heart over.
He remembers walks on the beach, when everything he said was truth.
He remembers lectures on how to behave when meeting her date, and
And, her first serious boyfriend.

He remembers always watching the clock, when she was out.
He remembers sticky baby kisses that turned to teenage "Hi Fi's"
and then, lady-like hugs with a just a brush of a kiss on his cheek.

He yearns to tell her to always be happy.
He wants to tell her how much he loves her,
But the words seem to be caught somewhere deep within him.
So much time has gone by, So many missed opportunities.

So he strides back into the house – a man with a purpose.
And amidst the giggles, perfume, hairspray, lace and satin,
He taps his child on the shoulder,
Pushes a wisp of hair from her brow
And says, "I love you..
Don't ever forget the guy who gave you your first kiss."
As she says, "Oh Daddy...he knows she will never forget

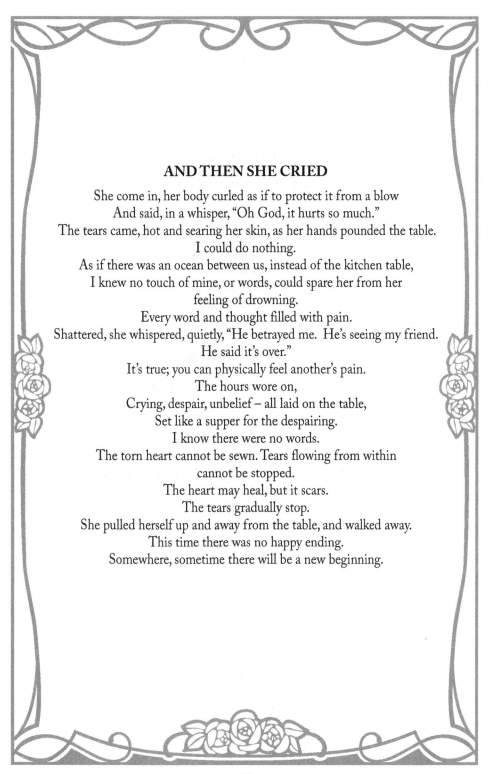

AND THEN SHE CRIED

She come in, her body curled as if to protect it from a blow
And said, in a whisper, "Oh God, it hurts so much."
The tears came, hot and searing her skin, as her hands pounded the table.
I could do nothing.
As if there was an ocean between us, instead of the kitchen table,
I knew no touch of mine, or words, could spare her from her
feeling of drowning.
Every word and thought filled with pain.
Shattered, she whispered, quietly, "He betrayed me. He's seeing my friend.
He said it's over."
It's true; you can physically feel another's pain.
The hours wore on,
Crying, despair, unbelief – all laid on the table,
Set like a supper for the despairing.
I know there were no words.
The torn heart cannot be sewn. Tears flowing from within
cannot be stopped.
The heart may heal, but it scars.
The tears gradually stop.
She pulled herself up and away from the table, and walked away.
This time there was no happy ending.
Somewhere, sometime there will be a new beginning.

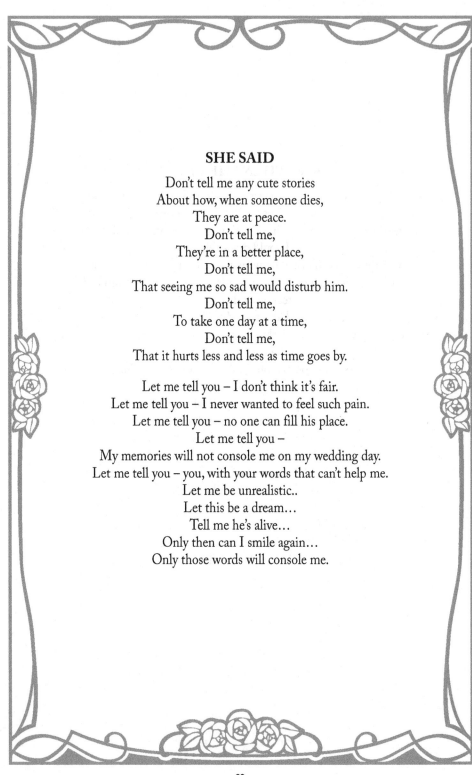

SHE SAID

Don't tell me any cute stories
About how, when someone dies,
They are at peace.
Don't tell me,
They're in a better place,
Don't tell me,
That seeing me so sad would disturb him.
Don't tell me,
To take one day at a time,
Don't tell me,
That it hurts less and less as time goes by.

Let me tell you – I don't think it's fair.
Let me tell you – I never wanted to feel such pain.
Let me tell you – no one can fill his place.
Let me tell you –
My memories will not console me on my wedding day.
Let me tell you – you, with your words that can't help me.
Let me be unrealistic..
Let this be a dream…
Tell me he's alive…
Only then can I smile again…
Only those words will console me.

GRANDMOTHER

To be a grandmother is a special gift.
A grandmother stands back and watches her beautiful grandchild grow.
She delights in every smile,
Melts with every hug and kiss,
She has a special place in this continuation of life,
And with all her heart and soul
She strives to fulfill her role.
Her arms are for hugging,
Her hands for wiping away tears,
Her eyes for seeing the world as her little one does,
Her lap for holding,
And, a heart full of a special, magical love.
She carries wonderful packages of lovely surprises
And pockets full of wondrous treats.
In the stillness of the night, when she's alone,
She thanks God for the gifts she has received,
The gift of grandchildren,
The gift of unconditional love.

LITTLE MISS COURTNEY

She makes me laugh
She sparkles like a diamond
Her eyes carry the wisdom of the ages.
She can hold a pet close to her heart,
Whisper in it's ear
And silently they laugh together.
She lights up the room she's in.
She lights up my life.
I believe she's been here before
And is here to teach all those she encounters,
How to love, understand, kindness and goodness
and to always have joy.
She is love and joy,
She owns my heart.

FOR MY GRANDDAUGHTER ALLISON

On a day that seemed to be filled with
Magical pink, fluffy clouds,
Sprinkled with silvery stardust and a dazzling rainbow;
In a brightly colored cart,
Guarded by beautiful fairy godmothers,
Pulled by a team of glorious white unicorns,
Allison arrived...

As the mystery of life enfolds,
Giving us little glimmers of the
Magnificence of the Universe,
I found myself completely in awe,
Having witnessed the miracle
Of the arrival of my grandchild,
Who has chosen to share this life experience with us.
Looking at this wisp of God's glorious creation
I felt my heart filled with
What the poets call, "Unconditional Love."

A perfect little child with upturned nose
And heart shaped lips.
A wisp of heaven, with stardust filled eyes,
Unaware she has stolen my heart away..
I thanked God for this miracle,
And,
I thanked God again, for my children,
Who have always filled my heart
With "Unconditional Love." Agape!

ALLISON

There she is peeking out at me.
Sitting in front of my vanity mirror and putting on lipstick,
Dressing up in one of my dresses...all pinned up...
Tiny hands, thin - oh so thin arms...
Eyes so bright and beaming
A smile that would light the Universe...
Filled with make-believe dreams and stories.
My Allison....my first granddaughter...
How can one measure love?
She has taken my heart and filled it with love.
To see her run,
Hear her laugh,
Make jokes,
Dance around,
Wear a large white brimmed straw hat
And her pink dancing outfit,
Coming for a visit
Makes living worthwhile.
A mystical child, who knows many things from the past..
She has been in turn, a princess, a dancer, an actress,
She is beautiful beyond words
And gentle and understanding
To have her lean over and
Say to me, "I really love you Nana."
Makes life worth living.
All I can say is
Thank you God.

FOR TAYLOR

Hello, my precious little one.
On March 15, 1999,
You came peeking around
The curtain of heaven to be with us.
A beautiful child of God, full of beauty, health, happiness and joy.
You entered our lives, on a Golden Chariot, cushioned by fluffy pink clouds,
Bringing stardust and bright sunshine
That changed a snowy day into a day of summer.
Again I have seen the mystery of life enfold.
And the mystical magnificence of the Universe,
In awe, as I was privileged to witness the miracle of the arrival
of my second grandchild.

This beautiful princess who chose us to share this life experience with us.

Seeing this perfect expression of God,
I again felt my heart lift with thanksgiving and love

A beautiful little child with golden hair and turned up nose,
Full of grace, beauty, health and peace.
And I again sit in wonder, thinking how much love one can feel.
With great humility and joy, I thanked God for this miracle,
I thanked God again, for my son, Brian, this child's father, and,
Cindy, this child's mother,
And for you, my princess, I give my heart full of unconditional love. Agape!

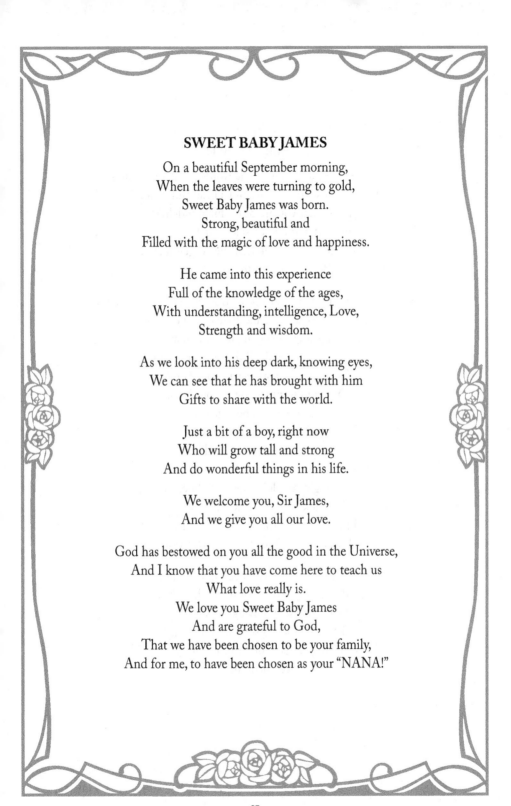

SWEET BABY JAMES

On a beautiful September morning,
When the leaves were turning to gold,
Sweet Baby James was born.
Strong, beautiful and
Filled with the magic of love and happiness.

He came into this experience
Full of the knowledge of the ages,
With understanding, intelligence, Love,
Strength and wisdom.

As we look into his deep dark, knowing eyes,
We can see that he has brought with him
Gifts to share with the world.

Just a bit of a boy, right now
Who will grow tall and strong
And do wonderful things in his life.

We welcome you, Sir James,
And we give you all our love.

God has bestowed on you all the good in the Universe,
And I know that you have come here to teach us
What love really is.
We love you Sweet Baby James
And are grateful to God,
That we have been chosen to be your family,
And for me, to have been chosen as your "NANA!"

KELLY
October 15, 2000

Someone wrote a song with the words, "Polka Dots and
Moonbeams wrapped around a beautiful dream."
That's what you are beautiful grandchild.
Pink and white, soft and tender, sparkling blue eyes, a tiny nose
And a dimpled cheek that the Angels kissed
Before you left to come to us.

A daddy and mommy's dream come true. And a Nana's delight.
One more precious child to love and cherish.
You are a gift bringing us joy and awe.
A gift we will cherish all the days of our lives.
As you take your place in your family,
You add so much love to our lives,
We have again been blessed,
And I am especially blessed.
I get to give the hugs and kisses
When mommy and daddy think you are naughty.
I get to give the lollipops and chocolates,
Lipsticks and high-heel play shoes,
I get to play all the make-believe games
I know you are really Princess Aurora

Mommy and daddy have to be mommy and daddy
And they love you with their whole heart,
I can spoil you only like a Nana can.
I thank God for sending you to us.
An for giving Nana another beautiful grandchild
To love unconditionally.

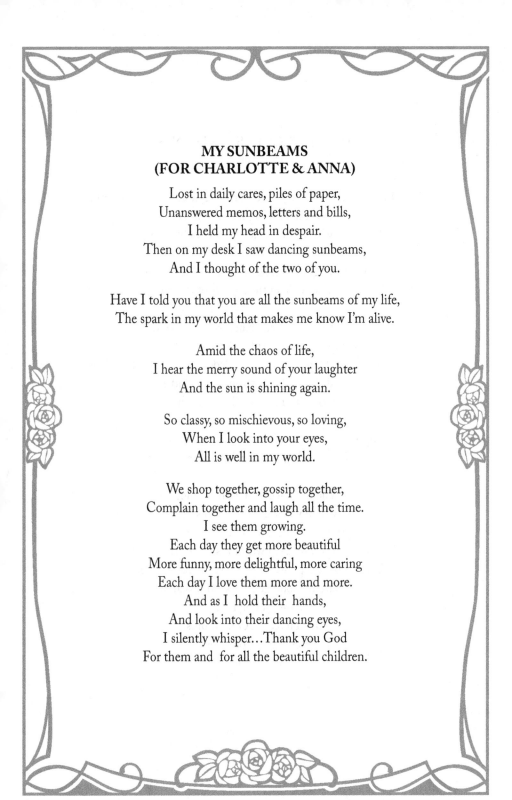

MY SUNBEAMS
(FOR CHARLOTTE & ANNA)

Lost in daily cares, piles of paper,
Unanswered memos, letters and bills,
I held my head in despair.
Then on my desk I saw dancing sunbeams,
And I thought of the two of you.

Have I told you that you are all the sunbeams of my life,
The spark in my world that makes me know I'm alive.

Amid the chaos of life,
I hear the merry sound of your laughter
And the sun is shining again.

So classy, so mischievous, so loving,
When I look into your eyes,
All is well in my world.

We shop together, gossip together,
Complain together and laugh all the time.
I see them growing.
Each day they get more beautiful
More funny, more delightful, more caring
Each day I love them more and more.
And as I hold their hands,
And look into their dancing eyes,
I silently whisper…Thank you God
For them and for all the beautiful children.

HE'S HERCULES & ADONIS
(For Peter)

The Lion roared in August and our Hercules/Adonis was born.
He came fighting into the world,
Bringing with him, memories of lives lived before

Charming, strong, sensitive and courageous
He came with all the aspects of the lion.

As a baby he lifted chairs with one hand,
Climbed up stairs and explored every part of his lair.
A wise, thoughtful child, possessing knowledge of other lands and events.
Tall and strong, he confronts each and every
task with his lion-like strength.

Sports are his forte, however when you see him
on the ocean, surfing, you see he and the sea are one.

When you see him with his mom,
When you see him with his dog,
When you see him with his special cousins,
When you see him with his special friends,
You see the deep love and loyalty he has for them.
Strength, Courage and Kindness all in
one young boy,
Our Hercules, Our Adonis,
Peter, king of our world.
(Love Nana)

A REAL LONG ISLAND LITTLE PRINCESS

They call her Shannon, but I know she is really
A princess from another time.

Beautiful face, gentle spirit, filled
with giggles and laughter.

She's the baby, and still cuddles with her mom,
Adores and bosses her dad,
Thinks her nana is from another planet
and
Gets anything she wants from her sisters,
who are her handmaidens.
Filled with joy, great in sports,
Lots of best friends,
One is the most special – Danny!

Each day is filled with sunshine when you are with her,
She is what makes life so worth living.
I thank God…for giving us this beautiful Princess.

Love Nana

FOR MY BROTHER

I knew a little boy once.
His knees were cut, and his hair was mussed.
In one hand he held a piece of wood for whittling,
and a drum stick in the other.
He had a spark of devilment in his eyes and a heart full of love and laughter,
That you just had to smile when you saw him.
He had holes in shoes, …but he didn't care. His shirt was dirty…
but he didn't care.
He had a dream that he had to pursue. This he knew at five.
He fought dragons with wooden swords and slew armies with a wooden gun.
He flew to Mars in his imaginary plane,
and make stacks of wood his mountain.
And there he reigned as a successful warrior and king.
Within him he had a bubbling fount of laughter and mischief.
His delight was to scare his sister and make her cry.
Then, like the knights of old – he would save her.
He's still trying to save her.
Lonely, yes. Did anyone know – no. Did anyone care – I don't know.
He grew up by himself. Self-sufficient since birth.
Genius hid behind his dirty face.
He knew the secrets of the ages and they were there in his eyes.
But he never told. He just went on.
Strong – yes with a strength that comes from within him
And has never wavered nor diminished.

Following the mission of his life, he left home and hearth for his dream.
This he found in regimental organized ideas and ideals.
Never resting, never stopping, always searching, he pursued his goals.
His talent for music began with a small drum,
And a lonely man who taught him how to beat on it.
Now he conducts an entire orchestra.

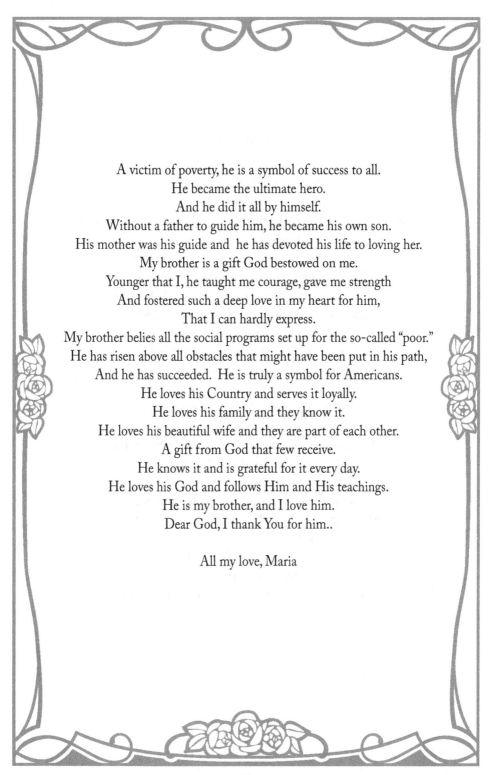

A victim of poverty, he is a symbol of success to all.
He became the ultimate hero.
And he did it all by himself.
Without a father to guide him, he became his own son.
His mother was his guide and he has devoted his life to loving her.
My brother is a gift God bestowed on me.
Younger that I, he taught me courage, gave me strength
And fostered such a deep love in my heart for him,
That I can hardly express.
My brother belies all the social programs set up for the so-called "poor."
He has risen above all obstacles that might have been put in his path,
And he has succeeded. He is truly a symbol for Americans.
He loves his Country and serves it loyally.
He loves his family and they know it.
He loves his beautiful wife and they are part of each other.
A gift from God that few receive.
He knows it and is grateful for it every day.
He loves his God and follows Him and His teachings.
He is my brother, and I love him.
Dear God, I thank You for him..

All my love, Maria

MY BABY SISTER

Can you believe it?
I loved her before she was born.
It only increased when I saw her.
Pink and white, curly hair and a tiny mouth, that I was sure smiled at me.
In all these years it never changed.
I am sure we were together in another life time.
Toddling along at one year, riding her bike at 5,
Crying at my wedding, staying with me all the time.
She grew up with my children, as one of them.
I watched her as she grew through,
high school, college and when she married.
Serious, funny, bossy (yes), wonderful (always).
She was my anchor when I needed someone.
Until this moment, there is a bond so strong
It cannot be explained.
She's a successful woman, wonderful mother and a
caring aunt and grandmother.
When I am lost and lonely, she is there.
When I am wrong, she never chastises me,
When I am successful, she is right beside me cheering.
I still call her "baby sister,"
She is my borrowed "first child."
She is my everything.
And every day, I thank God, for she is my blessing.

Random Thoughts

MARILYN

Silk and satin
White clouds,
Frosted glasses,
Utrillo and Sinatra.
Dazzling fire, scented candles,
Long summer days,
Cooled by vanilla ice cream.
Soft hands dipped into clear brooks
The crunch of autumn leaves
Under summer sandals.
A sigh, a smile
A tear-stained face hidden by billows of golden hair.
A farewell kiss, then she's gone.
Goodbye Marilyn.

PEOPLE IN YOUR SPACE

People.
Take up your Space.
Chew up parts of your life.
Talk till your head aches.
So involved in their petty problems.
Never listening.
Only spewing out selfish,
Depression and words.
Until you feel you're
Drowning in their so-called humanness.
People.
Do they,
Ever think
You too
Have something to say?

MEMORIES COME TO HAUNT ME ON LONG, LONELY NIGHTS

THE DAY YOU LEFT
You kissed me goodbye,
Closed the door and walked away,
And my heart broke.

SHARE YOUR HEART WITH ME
Speak to me in tender tones,
Walk with me on golden beaches.
Sail with me on emerald seas,
Glide with me on silver ice.
Dance with me on pink clouds,
Dream with me on balmy, summer nights.
Share your heart with me,
I have already given you all of mine.

INVISIBLE ME
A turn of the head,
A glimpse of a blue jacket,
The scent of after-shave lingering notes of a song
The tight knot in my throat when I think of you,
You're "too" cheerful hello
Feeling my spirit strain and reach out to you,
Knowing you are totally oblivious to what I feel
Leaves me with a sense of despair.

ALWAYS YOUNG
We never change
Within our being, we are,, forever,
As we were,
That beautiful summer day.

THE CHILDREN OF OYSTER BAY, LONG ISLAND

Today is Halloween
Today I saw the children of Oyster Bay..
Ah yes, the children of Oyster Bay.
Wealth is in their every feature.
No strong Italian or Irish heritage,
Rather a washed, clean image of Americana – Of Oyster Bay.

Like the countryside where they live,
They are pristine.
Even their tears seem somehow different.
No wailing, nor runny noses,
Each cry or tear refined in its bearing, by its bearer.
The children of wealth,
It oozes from every pore.

One would like to think that children are the same everywhere,
But that is not true.
These children are somehow a bit more delicate,
Tissue paper thin,
Almost fearful of annoying mom or dad by being a child.

In a rare moment I saw Tinkerbelle hug her dad,
Then he twirled her in the air,
And her laughter soared in the valley –
But for just a moment,
Then the mask came down,
As he politely deposited her on the ground,
And Tinkerbelle quietly stood by his side – once again –
A perfect Oyster Bay child.

Selectivism begins early in Oyster Bay,
And very few are allowed into the charmed circle.
So very much they have,
One would think – But looking on, I see so little,
For they will never be able to have that "best friend"

They can only have the "right friend."
Cushioned by manners and wealth,
They are sheltered from feeling,
Stopped from being children.
The children of Oyster Bay – are so beautiful,
But so very lonely, and in a sense, deprived.
But God is merciful and they don't know that.

THE GATE TO MY MIND HAS OPENED

Suddenly the gates to my mind have opened.
Now, I can write again
A part of my mind has been revitalized
Too long my mind has been like a dry desert.
Today the healing rains came
and turned that desert
Into a green garden filled with the flowers
Of words and feelings.
I an alive again,
I am grateful.
I have many questions and few answers.
So I say to the muses
That once again fill my mind and soul,
Thank you!

THE STAR

I felt lonely tonight.
Then I looked up at the sky
And saw a star.
I knew you were looking at the same star,
And in that moment, we were together,
And I was no longer lonely.

RAIN

I haven't seen anything so beautiful in a long time..
As the crystal beads of rain cling to the pine tree
Outside my kitchen window.
The steady rain affects not at all the pine,
Yet the oak and maple droop from their burden of water.
They seem to sway and beg for the rain to cease.
There are different types of rain
Just as there are different types of people.
There is the steady, unrelenting, harsh rain,
Whose only purpose seems to be is to wet and flood the land,
Pressing upon the earth and human mind its steady, soaking wetness.
There is the light, gentle rain that kisses the grass, soil and trees lightly,
Just enough to fulfill their thirst and wash their surfaces.
There is the hot, fierce, capricious summer rain that rages for minutes,
Soaks the body and land, then runs speedily away.
Each raindrop, feels like a kiss from God.

INSPIRATION

Again I look to you for inspiration,
And again, you do not fail me.
I watched you petting your kitten,
And I thought how soft the strong hands are
That hold a bay gelding in tow.
You speak to me of ordinary things,
Full of animation, and I imagined you three years old,
Filled with excitement upon seeing your puppy.
Child, Child,
You have given me so much joy,
Child, Child, I love you.

HAPPY BIRTHDAY

This day is special, because this day is yours.
It's a glorious day,
The sun is shining, the daisies are dancing with joy,
Because they know it's your birthday.
Happy Birthday!

AS I SIT HERE ALONE, I THINK

Tinkling glasses,
Soft music,
Spilled wine,
Stained tablecloth,
A love ended,
A stain that never comes out.
Pain that never goes away.

JOY

Joy is of the moment,
The softness of a baby's new fuzzy hair
Touching your face
The alertness of your heart, 'When a child asks
"Nana – Can I tell you something?"

SHALLOW PEOPLE

Stop criticizing
No matter how shallow some may be,
Do you know,
God loves them anyway?
I don't know why,
But then again, God is wiser than I.

BROTHERHOOD

Come, take my hand, and we will take a magical trip to many lands....
We will glory in the blue waters of Hawaii,
We will glow in the chill of Norway's fiords,
We will be enriched by the culture of Greece,
We will cling together in the mysteries of the Orient..
And, we will be revitalized in the energy of America.

Let us imagine a world,
Where everyone is the same color
Everyone speaks the same language,
Everyone has the same religion.

It isn't hard to do,
If you are my brother, - you do it everyday.
If I fall, you don't look to see what color I am before you
help me up.
If I cry, You understand - no matter what language I speak.
If I pray, I know I am heard - no matter what faith
I follow.
It is up to us -
To be blinded to color.
To be deafened to languages.
To pray - whatever Church we may be in.

The hungry people of Africa do not look to see what color the
hand is that holds the bowl of food.
The yellow boat people do not ask the nationality of the sailors who help them.
The crying orphan children of India do not know that Mother Theresa
Is a Catholic,

The fleeing Jews blessed the homes of the Lutheran Norwegians
who sheltered them.
And so, it is our responsibility:
To hold the crying child - no matter what her color.
To feed the elderly woman - no matter what her nationality.
To give water to the parched man - no matter his religion.

Take my hand,
We will travel this road of life as brothers,
And make possible the world John Lennon sang of:

"Imagine there's no countries,
Nothing to kill or die for,
Imagine all the people living for today,
You may think I'm a dreamer,
But I'm not the only one.
If everyone would join us,
The world would be one."

WORDS, WORDS, WORDS

Words close in the throat
Words that will never be spoken
Never spoken because the speaker
Can never be sure of their reception.
Will they understand?
Will anyone understand?
Sometimes so many things are choked up inside
That one feels smothered.
But who to tell?
The phone rings and you become again
Part of the world.
Shallow.
No one will ever know the churning,
The sadness and pain
That goes on in the Mind
All the speeches that have been composed
And the quest for understanding
Falls on fallow ground.
Because no one cares.

RANDOM THOUGHTS WHILE I SIT ALONE

FAME

Fame is like a warm summer breeze
That caresses the face,
Cools the body
And leaves us
As we dream of its next assault.

GOODBY AGAIN

Sometimes life seems to be a series of
"So-longs and Good-byes"
Not only literally, but in theory.
"Hi – how are you?"
"Fine – OK – I'll see you."
"Have a good day – see you later"
On and On
Proving we must find and hold on to ourselves.
We must be special to one's self.
So we too can also say "So long"
And get on with the business of living.

WHEN THINGS GO BADLY

Sometimes the night feels ten nights long.

MOMENTS

How delicate are the moments of life are...
Like the petals of a sun-kissed flower.

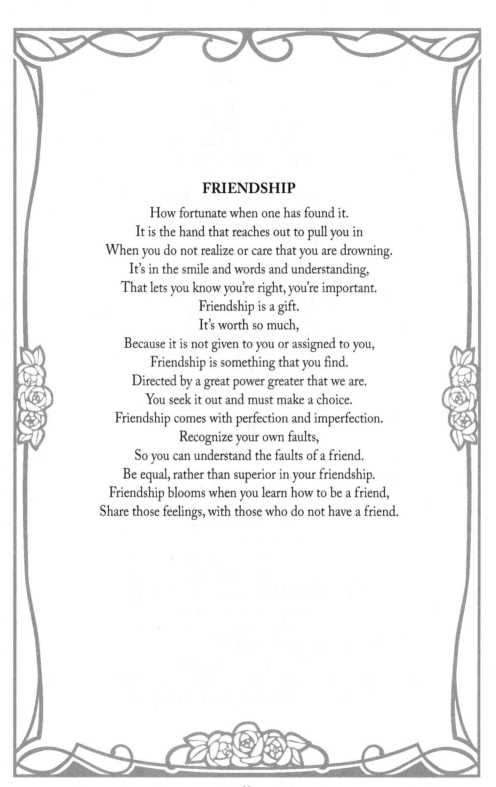

FRIENDSHIP

How fortunate when one has found it.
It is the hand that reaches out to pull you in
When you do not realize or care that you are drowning.
It's in the smile and words and understanding,
That lets you know you're right, you're important.
Friendship is a gift.
It's worth so much,
Because it is not given to you or assigned to you,
Friendship is something that you find.
Directed by a great power greater that we are.
You seek it out and must make a choice.
Friendship comes with perfection and imperfection.
Recognize your own faults,
So you can understand the faults of a friend.
Be equal, rather than superior in your friendship.
Friendship blooms when you learn how to be a friend,
Share those feelings, with those who do not have a friend.

APOLOGY..

How do you say "Forgive me?"
Lying in bed at night,
One can compose beautiful notes and words.
But in the harsh light of morning,
In the reality of daily life,
You find you can't say, "Forgive Me."
It just isn't enough.
You may have to explain
Why you want to be forgiven,
And you don't want to do that,
The two words are enough, for you maybe,
But not for the one who is hurt.
Can't they understand?
The words come from your inner being,
And the explanation comes
From the reality of what has occurred,
And then, loses all its meaning.

EGO – THE BARRIER

What is this thing we call Ego.
Ah, many definitions exist,
In truth, Ego is the destroyer.
Ego prevents one from saying, "I love you."
Ego wishes only to be "loved."
Ego creates anger within.
And takes all slights personally,
Ego stands between you and your real self.
The world would be a place of continuous joy
If the Ego could be controlled.
It is the Ego that prevents us from trusting
Trust is the master key to all the good that life offers.
Release Ego, be the real you.
Then the Master Key to all joy will be in your hand
And the door will be opened to all you dreamed of.

AN INDIAN SPEAKS ON FAITH.

You asked me my Indian Name,
I tell you, Sweet Bird, Flying Eagle, Bright Feather
Than you ask me my Christian name, and I tell you, '
Mary, Thomas Peter.

You ask me – "Why do you have two names?"
And I tell you this story that my father's father handed down to me.

It is written in the history of the Proud Indian Nation,
That one day from far shores, strange men came.
We fed them - and they took our food,
And we knew hunger.
We gave them water, and they muddied our streams and now we thirst.
We gave them corn, and they took our land
And we began to wander.
They brought to us – guilt
They brought to us – sickness
They brought to us – treachery

And just as we were desolate and dying,
The hand of Manitou touched us,
And His breath hastened the sails of ships of
Good men and women.
They came to feed us the bread of life.
They touched and healed our wounds
They cared for our babies and women,
And they raised our souls from the dead caused by despair.
They came who came in the name of a man called Jesus.
He too had suffered at the hands of evil men.
They touched our lives with love,
With a gift that weaves us together like fine linen cloth.

A gift that has brightened our dark cold nights,
And has wiped the tears from the mother's faces
And they gave courage to our Braves.
They healed us because they lived by the simplest words ever spoken,
"Love One Another As I Have Love You."

THOUGHTS IN AUTUMN

RELEASE ME

You impale me with your devotion.
You smother me with your love,
You stifle my spirit with your needs,
You trapped me by marrying me

YOUR SMILE

Your smile is like
The feeling of sand
Warmed by the sun.

LOOK BEHIND THE STRENGTH

A woman, so vulnerable to the capriciousness of life,
Living a lie that she is strong.
Doesn't anyone see the sad, lost child,
Hiding behind the polished, take charge veneer?

YOUR EYES REVEAL

Your eyes reveal the
love you hide.

TRANSFORMATION

Standing in front of my mirror this morning,
I put on a rainbow
And watched myself transform
As I entered the magical, mystical world of make-believe.

Glowing a russet color, turning my head,
I became Rita Hayworth's - Gilda..

Tossing a Black cape over my shoulder,
I stood tall and strong,
Maria Callas - singing Turandot..

Quick strides around the room,
Nervously trying to decide what to wear,
I became Bette Davis in" Now Voyager,"

Calming down, I placed a soft, emerald scarf around my neck
The color of Gene Tierney's eyes..
And slipped into a white silk shirt and slacks,
Struck a pose and saw in the mirror of my mind,
Marilyn Monroe and Jean Harlow.

One last look into my magic mirror -
And around my head
I saw all the magnificent colors of the rainbow,
And somewhere far in the distance I heard a voice gently singing
"If happy little bluebirds fly
Above the rainbow, Why, Oh Why - Can't I?"
Oh Judy - how we loved you.

THE FOG WITHIN

Looking out the window
I saw the fog.
It was like another world.
Although safe and warm,
Sheltered within the haven of my home,
A storm was going on in the safe house within me.
All the pain,
Days and nights of worry and loneliness..
Unspeakable words!
Not to be said aloud,
One must maintain the smiling,
Stoic face of a civilized human being.
And so, you begin to drift so far within
Your own voice sounds like an echo...
And you pray for the day the fog will lift.

THE WRITER

A blank sheet of paper beacons,
Words flow and stain the page
fulfilling the mind
Satisfying the outpouring of one's deepest thoughts
That are held within the heart.
Spewing things for others to see and read.
Those who do not wish to listen to the words,
However, when written upon a page,
They become "genius"
And, they say,
"Oh how wonderful"
As the writer struggles with their sanity.

1762 SEDDON STREET

As I look back,
I remember when sunshine poured into my life –
My days at 1762 Seddon Street, grandma & grandpa's house.

The years have never lessened the glow of the hours spent there,
Warm and safe with grandma and grandpa.

I remember,
Clean fresh air blowing through the open windows of grandma's house,
Strong Italian coffee, crusty toasted bread and fresh whipped butter.
White wash on the line, drying in the sun.
Grandma's arms, warm, strong, working arms, arms that hugged two
lonely children.

I remember opening the "Branda"
The cot grandpa slept in when he had rheumatism attacks.
The silver bird singing in the music box from Germany
My uncle brought home after the war.
The three faceted mirror on grandma's vanity.

Those mysterious stairs leading up to the attic, Stealing up there to
search through the trunks,
And being locked in that attic by my naughty brother.

I remember
The smell of fresh crushed grapes oozing up from grandpa's wine cellar.
The trunk in the unheated back room – full of mystery inspiring
our wonderful imaginations.
Laying on the grass, watching the clouds change into castles.
The RCA Victorola with "His Master's Voice" on the cover.
Grandpa's coat pockets filled with dimes and nickels.
The wonderful pot-bellied stove
that warmed us as nothing since has.
The wash board and brown soap.
The ice-box – which never left its place of prominence
Even when the refrigerator came.

Looking out the kitchen window and seeing the fig trees,
Watching grandpa wrap those treasured trees – a touch of his native land.

I remember standing on the back porch and smelling the peaches,
as I walked with grandma – listening as she pulled peach leaves and
cracked them with her fingers.

I remember every Summer morning,
Six A.M. and Grandpa in his vegetable garden,
This old soldier carrying buckets of water to his beloved plants.
There were cats on the woodpile
And my brother on the woodpile.
My grandma's warm hands wiping and soothing away all our tears.
My uncles' beautiful cars,
Meatballs, sauce, stuffed artichokes and ham sandwiches,
Grandma's gentle hands bathing my sore legs.
Her beautiful Grecian nose.

I remember my uncles' friends with names like Gigi, Fatso and Handsome
I remember the adopted twins in the Delaney House
Where the "rich" Irish people lived.
The taste of mello-rolls and pipe licorice,

Molly and Samuel who owned the corner deli, who were friends
of my grandpa, he, who spoke broken English and they who spoke Yiddish.

The beauty of the Protestant Church across the avenue,
The delight of buying comic books and penny note books,
My brother whittling and playing soldier.
My brother – all three feet of him – walking atop the picket fence,
My grandpa, the once "real" soldier chasing this daring whittling young "soldier."
As he swung on a rope above the woodpile.

They called it a shack.
To us, it was a haven, a safety shelter,
A warmth, security, it was 1762 Seddon Street where we were loved,
And where we learned to love.
I remember and will never forget,
Grateful to God for those precious days,
Those experiences, and for my beloved grandma, grandpa,
Uncle Jim and Uncle Dan
And for the fruit, the bread, the sun and most of all,
the love.

OLD GLORY SPEAKS

I saw them marching one by one,
In army fatigues, sweat-stained, covered with desert sand.
I saw drawn faces, wet feet, sloshing through swamps in Vietnam.
I saw them hunched over, blowing on their hands for warmth,
Wrapped in wool, trying to keep warm in the hills of Korea.
I saw them slashing vines in the jungles of Guadalcanal –
And the others,
Running with guns raised in the cold, wet, dead of night onto Anzio Beach.
Never to return.
On and on, lines of men.
I saw them in tinny helmets, gas-masked faces,
The "Yankee Doodle Dandies" of World War I,
The line was unending.
I saw young confident Confederate and Union soldiers,
Fighting – American against American.
The line continued,
There were young farmers brandishing homemade arms,
Moving along the shores of the Potomac and hills of Valley Forge,
So many, So many there, so many gone, only a memory to loved ones.
Looking ahead,
I saw the young soldiers in Bosnia, the young marines in Somalia
The navy seals in Afganistan..bodies torn, nerves shattered;
And so it begins once more and continues on and on
War - What lessons have been learned? What gain can there be in loss?
What joy can be found in sorrow? What peace forged in fighting?
They raise me over their heads, march with me at the forefront,
Proud and brave.
The "Cause" Freedom,
And I asked, "Tell me with is the Cause?'"
And from the hollow hills and the faceless men came –
No Answer.

All The Beautiful Moments

FOREVER YOUNG
(Dedicated to Paula)

Oh God! – I'm so grateful for the moments we shared,
Walks on the beach, sloshing in the sand,
Midnight snacks and chocolate egg-creams,
Lots of tea.

Days in Florida – hot sun, Coppertone and L'Amant perfume.
Eyes connecting, winking over the heads of our dates.
Running out of gas at midnight in Miami,
With the sky glorious violet and the palms swaying.
Years of study, housework and children,
Disappear in a flash when we're together.
Hair in place, lashes fluttering, giggles and hearty laughs.
Successful women, loving friends – Forever Young.

And I will always keep in my heart,
The memory of seeing your beautiful face
Deep in prayer as you sat by my hospital bed.

And the music continues, and the laughter lingers in the air,
We talk and talk, and the years pass,
And we remain Forever Young.

MAGICAL MOMENTS

When I'm alone with my thoughts,
I am with you again,
Seeing your smile, hearing your laugh,
Feeling your touch, sharing your wine,
Touching your face,
Cherishing the memories...
When we shared those magical moments.

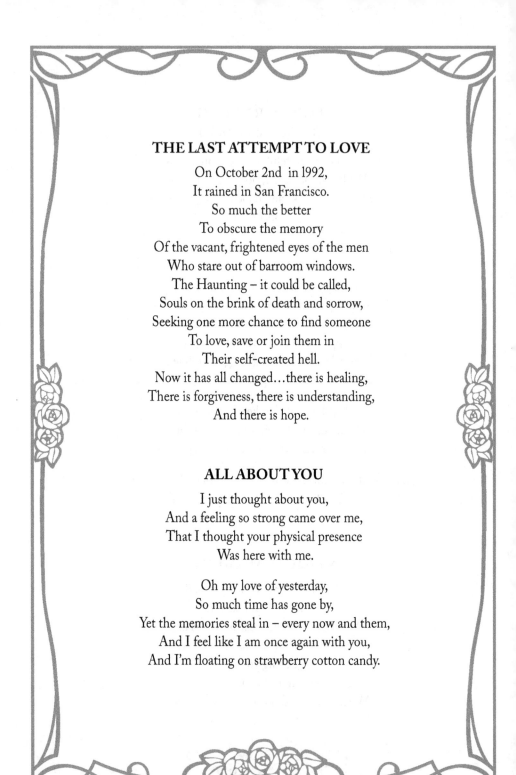

THE LAST ATTEMPT TO LOVE

On October 2nd in 1992,
It rained in San Francisco.
So much the better
To obscure the memory
Of the vacant, frightened eyes of the men
Who stare out of barroom windows.
The Haunting – it could be called,
Souls on the brink of death and sorrow,
Seeking one more chance to find someone
To love, save or join them in
Their self-created hell.
Now it has all changed…there is healing,
There is forgiveness, there is understanding,
And there is hope.

ALL ABOUT YOU

I just thought about you,
And a feeling so strong came over me,
That I thought your physical presence
Was here with me.

Oh my love of yesterday,
So much time has gone by,
Yet the memories steal in – every now and them,
And I feel like I am once again with you,
And I'm floating on strawberry cotton candy.

EXPRESSIONS OF LOVE

Reaching over, I touched her hand,
How soft I thought
Although she's not young anymore.
And I silently whispered I love you Mom.
Last night I heard in the distance the echo of his hearty laugh,
And I silently whispered, I love you Dad.

She stood center stage
All dressed up in lace, ribbons and shiny tap shoes,
All three years of her,
And joined the others – out of step!
And I silently whispered – I love you my child.

As he bent his head down, I saw my tall, blonde son
Place the ring on his beloved's finger,
And I silently whispered – I love you my son.

What is love?
It is God touching your spirit
Inspiring a feeling of such pure, perfect joy,
That you momentarily soar with the angels,
And you can only experience
When you give your love away.

EVERY WEDNESDAY AT 3:00 PM

I see her standing at the bus stop every Wednesday,
Shoulders slumped, shopping bag in hand.
Brown skin gleaming, fatigue etched in the eyes,
The cleaning lady.

Go down any suburban street at three o'clock- on Wednesday,
and you will see her. Days spent cleaning,
catering to another woman's whims and criticism.
Why you say? At this age you ask?

She had a dream that drove her. She never wanted to see
her son or daughter have to stand at a bus stop every Wednesday.
Now her son is a doctor, her daughter a lawyer.
So, why does she continue cleaning strangers
bathrooms and bedrooms, having achieved that dream?
Because she never wants to be a "burden" to the doctor and lawyer.
So she continues to clean the lady's kitchen and dining room,
Scrubs the floors and irons the stranger's shirts.
And prays silently to her God for strength.
She receives that strength, and inwardly smiles,
Knowing that her God is always right beside her
Helping her, consoling her and cleaning the stranger's
bathroom and bedrooms with her.
God not only has her back,
God carries her mop, dust rags and brooms.
Now, that my friends is FAITH!

A BLANK SHEET OF PAPER

A blank sheet of paper beckons
For words to flow and stain its page.
Fulfilling the mind,
Satisfying the outpouring of the deepest part of the heart.
Spewing things for others to see and read.
The same others who do not wish to hear them
But written upon the page
They become as genius and
"Oh how wonderful!!"

THE DANCE OF LIFE

We clapped, we turned,
We changed partners in a sweet roundel

I soared; I flew, folded like a swan
En Pointe.

They clapped, they tapped,
They sang Gypsy words,
Skirts flowing
Boots clicking
Flamenco is alive!

Barely touching,
We glided around the floor,
Perfect movement, perfect form
Sailing together on the golden ballroom floor
Each person involved, each muscle tensed
The Mind dancing
The Soul in Bliss
All comes together
In the Dance of life! Ole!

THE GOLDEN CHILD

Some years a girl-child was born.
This child was full of light, beauty and dreams.
As she grew – there were those who tried to darken that light
And trample on her dreams.
Momentarily they may have seemed to succeed.

But when a Golden Child comes to be among us,
No one can really dim their golden light.
For this child counts the stars each night,
Making sure they are all there.

You will see her looking over her shoulder
Winking at the moon.
She shares the secrets of time.
She glories in the warmth of the sun,
And feels most at home when she gazes at puffy, white clouds.
And so we thrill when we hear her sweet voice
Humming bars of a yet unwritten melody,
And feel the yearning to run barefoot in the grass,
Dive fearlessly into the sea,
And soar with eagles.
She is the golden gift of life,
We are she.

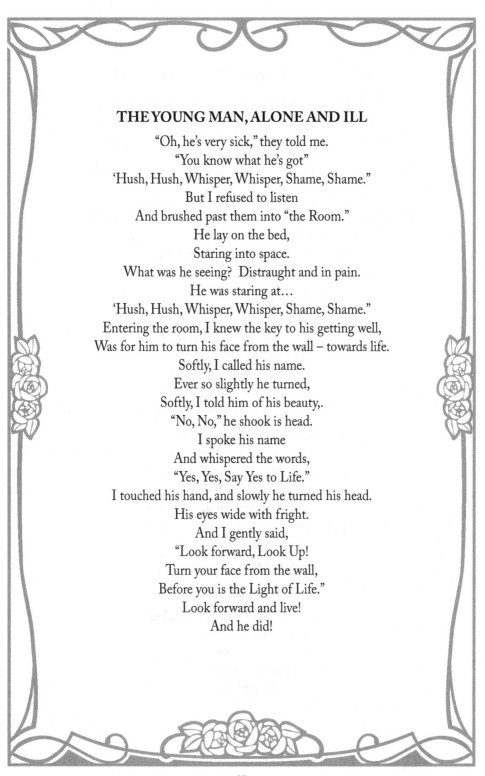

THE YOUNG MAN, ALONE AND ILL

"Oh, he's very sick," they told me.
"You know what he's got"
'Hush, Hush, Whisper, Whisper, Shame, Shame."
But I refused to listen
And brushed past them into "the Room."
He lay on the bed,
Staring into space.
What was he seeing? Distraught and in pain.
He was staring at…
'Hush, Hush, Whisper, Whisper, Shame, Shame."
Entering the room, I knew the key to his getting well,
Was for him to turn his face from the wall – towards life.
Softly, I called his name.
Ever so slightly he turned,
Softly, I told him of his beauty,.
"No, No," he shook is head.
I spoke his name
And whispered the words,
"Yes, Yes, Say Yes to Life."
I touched his hand, and slowly he turned his head.
His eyes wide with fright.
And I gently said,
"Look forward, Look Up!
Turn your face from the wall,
Before you is the Light of Life."
Look forward and live!
And he did!

AWAKENING FROM THE DEEP SLEEP

Without warning, I was plunged down into the depths
Where only despair, loneliness, anger, and tears live.
In that dark place, I lay as if I were on the bottom of the ocean,
and thought not of surfacing,
Like a dying swan, I wanted fold my wings, hide my head and rest.

Then with a force, that cannot be defined,
From the fathoms of the earth, with strength I didn't know existed,
They came, like an avenging army to rescue me.
Every word they spoke gave me courage,
Every gesture they extended gave me renewed strength.

They woke me from the deep sleep,
And I started to rise, slowly lifting my head,
I saw a legion of my loved ones,
Around before and behind me.
My children, mother, brother,
Sisters, uncles and grandparents,
United in one cause to lift me out of myself.

Like the Phoenix rising from the ashes,
I found myself climbing upward,
I wanted to breathe, and was alive once more.
Knowing, for all time,
That having been there in that dark place,
I would never seek to return there again.

ALONE AND THINKING

PROMISES

I promised myself one day I would laugh.
Then you taught me how.
You left me,
Now I've broken my promise,
I can't laugh.

WRITING FOR A LONELY LADY

All my life I have been searching for something to fill the void – within me.

That never seemed to be closed, what was it that I missed?

When did it start?

I think it was there the day I was born.

I remember the feeling as a child, always, just a little bit sad.

My smile, my laugh, my charm,

My talent was a cover-up to fool the world.

The world that only wanted to see the smiling, charming talented me.

Not the sad and lonely me.

I too did not want the world to see – the lonely me.

So I did the things all good children do.

I behaved correctly like all good girls do.

I grew and matured outwardly like all good young ladies do.

But the void became a gap and widened and struggled
and begged to be free.

And I, who for so many years – could ignore the void,

Looked into my suffering, loneliness and said—"Why Not"

Why can't I say: I need…I want…I desire..

Then I let the voice come out from deep within my being

And finally listened to its yearning.

I held it, and tried to sooth it.

I learned it couldn't be soothed, by me.

It needed somebody else. It needed the special glow that
comes when your hear,

You're lovely, I need You…Without You I cannot function.

Now, I will listen, I will search and try to capture what I longed for.

And always wonder, why did I wait so long?

MY DREAM

Yesterday I was young and full of hope
But fearful..
Today I am no longer young,
And I have no fear.
But…
I live with the knowledge
that I did not accomplish
The things I dreamed about.
Because I did not have
The courage to pursue them.
I followed the rules,
Did the Right Thing
And lost my dream.

ABOUT YOU

I have never loved before,
And I find it so difficult to
Give you – Myself.
But Myself is
Nothing without you.

MAGICAL MOMENTS

When I'm alone with my thoughts,
I am once again with you.
Seeing your smile, hearing your laugh,
Feeling your touch, sharing your wine,
Touching your face,
Cherishing the memories,
When we shared those magical moments.

RAINY DAY THOUGHTS

THE WRITER

She writes and feels the words
As they come from deep within her being.
The words stain the page, exposing the pain.
I pray, someday, I will write of joy.

FEAR

No need to look for fear, it exists within you.
It lives with you every moment,
Colors your world, chokes your attempts to laugh.
You try to speak and fear silences you.
Fall in love, and fear gives you doubt and mistrust.
You pray to your God, and fear speaks,
"Do you really believe anyone can help you?"
Let us annihilate fear, and bury it forever,
As we plants the seeds of life and trust.

SOMETIMES I WONDER

Sometimes I wonder what happens to me,
Can it be I don't really know how to love?
Because a sense of loneliness and isolation is always with me.

YOU LOVE ME?

Just for once
Listen to me!
There's nothing I want to say
I want you to understand me, without words,
When you can,
I'll believe you love me.

THINGS GO THROUGH MY MIND
Once you held me,
Once you listened to me.
Once you loved me.
You're gone.
I still love you.

REVELATION
Did you know Your eyes reveal
The love you hide.

YOUR SMILE
Your smile is like
The feeling of sand
Warmed by the sun.

IS THERE ANYONE HERE
Is there anyone here
To wipe away my tears?

KINDNESS
Did you know,
Your kindness today
Saved my sanity.

THE UNTRUTH

You swear your undying love,
And don't speak to me for weeks.
I thought you were my champion,
But you are like the facades used
On a Hollywood set.
I know this,
And still cannot understand why I care,
Or why I am so angry at myself.

LET TONIGHT BE FOREVER

Tonight for a while I own you.
Tomorrow will soon come
And with daybreak – heartbreak.
For in the hustle of the real world
It's no longer you and me –
But we and they and you and them.
Come back to me.
Let me feel again and live again
If only in the darkness.

DIMENSIONS OF TIME

Is it possible that we live
In a new dimension of time
Each lifetime?
Can it be that we can be born again
Back in time, in another century?

IT'S OVER

What do you do when love is over?
Do you tell him or her?
Or, do you live with your secret,
Knowing, each day your world is
Getting narrower and narrower?

ON A PLANE, ABOVE THE CLOUDS

Is this then heaven?
Here above the clouds,
Here you ask, why am I here?
To cry, to struggle, to give solace,
To love?
Many questions above the clouds,
No answers.

THINKING ALOUD

LAUGHTER

Laughter is a bright light.
Like a feather inside the body,
That causes it to ripple and vibrate,
Exploding into laughter.

WHAT IS LOVE?

Love has many faces,
It's on a child's tear stained face
On yours when you hold the child close.
It is in Grandma's twinkling eyes
As she remembers days past.
In your mother's voice
When you call her.
It's the feeling of relief
When a student's last exam is over.
It's in your lover's smile.
Love is you!

In The Silence

SITTING IN THE SILENCE

Sitting in the silence,
The mind wanders
And becomes like a child in a playground.

Looking this way and that way,
At all the many different things to play with.

Racing, Racing, Racing,
Scooting up the sliding pond,
Climbing the jungle gym,

Swinging on the swing,
Pumping higher and higher,
Until exhaustion settles in
And the swing goes back and forth in a natural rhythm,

And the child's gaze becomes fixed,
And slowly, slowly,

The child's eyes close in sleep.
How like the child we are,
When we go into the Silence.

LESSONS IN NATURE

Glimpse my friend, the evergreen outside your window.
Watch how it sways, bends and blends,
No matter what the weather.
When the rain beats down or the snow ladens its branches
And the summer sun scorches the earth,
And the winds of storms push and pull at it,
It changes not.
For it is in harmony with all the elements.
Many lessons may be learned from watching the evergreen.
The first lesson is Harmony.
The second is Steadfastness.
No matter what the circumstances,
The evergreen remains the same,
Green, sweet-smelling and strong.
The third lesson is Love.
The evergreen stretches out its branches in
Constant praise to its Creator,
Gives refuge to the birds,
And shelters the earth beneath its roots,
And in so doing,
Gives to us the greatest lesson we can learn.
Be in harmony
Stand steadfast
Trust and love,
And appear in all your beauty for the world to see
What God has created in you.

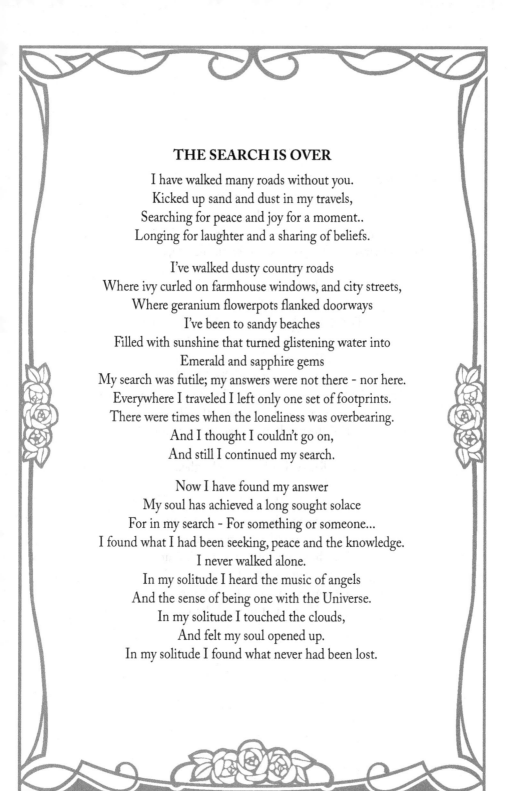

THE SEARCH IS OVER

I have walked many roads without you.
Kicked up sand and dust in my travels,
Searching for peace and joy for a moment..
Longing for laughter and a sharing of beliefs.

I've walked dusty country roads
Where ivy curled on farmhouse windows, and city streets,
Where geranium flowerpots flanked doorways
I've been to sandy beaches
Filled with sunshine that turned glistening water into
Emerald and sapphire gems
My search was futile; my answers were not there - nor here.
Everywhere I traveled I left only one set of footprints.
There were times when the loneliness was overbearing.
And I thought I couldn't go on,
And still I continued my search.

Now I have found my answer
My soul has achieved a long sought solace
For in my search - For something or someone...
I found what I had been seeking, peace and the knowledge.
I never walked alone.
In my solitude I heard the music of angels
And the sense of being one with the Universe.
In my solitude I touched the clouds,
And felt my soul opened up.
In my solitude I found what never had been lost.

THE LESSON

There is a lesson I learned long ago. My brother is myself.
Going past appearances, beneath the veneer of the years,
we are all the same.
When Mahatma Gandhi meditated, seated on God's good earth,
Deep in prayer, his prayer was not for one person, but for mankind.

When a child is born and held by his mother,
He knows not what color he or she is,
The child only knows only that it is   loved.
Later, much later, someone tells you,
"You are this…You are that..."
And so you must act accordingly, and you do.
As you look around, you know and that its time for change.
So turn your face towards the future,
Feel the winds of change on your skin.

Know that I am your brother,
For I am you, and you are me.
We are One.
Knowing this, how can I hurt you?
I would be hurting me.
So I reach out for your hand, touch your face,
As you rest your head on my shoulder,
And together we walk towards the future,
United in Love and Peace.

A MOMENT IN MEDITATION

We live life in moments.
The first moment we took breath
The first moment we walked
The first moment we spoke
The first moment we laughed
And the first moment we loved.

In Meditation this is the moment
The moment that lasts throughout eternity.
To know for one brief second
That you are in the presence
Of the most beautiful essence one can imagine
It is a feeling words cannot explain.

As one sits and silently turns inward to the One...
Like the scent of gardenias after the rain
And the magic of Christmas,
A feeling that cannot be described - wells within you.
In that moment you have touched God.

ALL ONE

There is a lesson I learned long ago.
My brother is myself.
Beneath the surface
We are all the same.

So turn your face towards me,
And know that I am your brother
For I am You and You are me.
We are One in the One.

Knowing this,
How can I hurt you?
I would be hurting me.

So I reach out for your hand,
I touch your face,
You rest your head on my shoulder
And together we walk towards the future,
Safe and Secure - All One.

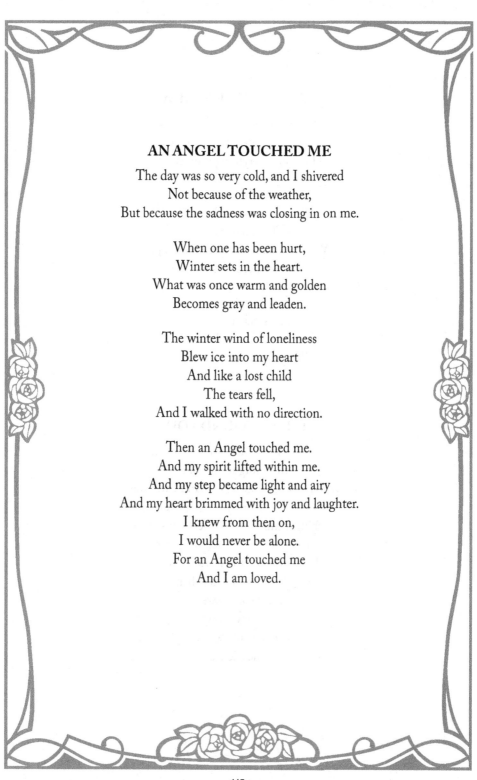

AN ANGEL TOUCHED ME

The day was so very cold, and I shivered
Not because of the weather,
But because the sadness was closing in on me.

When one has been hurt,
Winter sets in the heart.
What was once warm and golden
Becomes gray and leaden.

The winter wind of loneliness
Blew ice into my heart
And like a lost child
The tears fell,
And I walked with no direction.

Then an Angel touched me.
And my spirit lifted within me.
And my step became light and airy
And my heart brimmed with joy and laughter.
I knew from then on,
I would never be alone.
For an Angel touched me
And I am loved.

IT'S ALL IN THE VIEW

Soaring high above the clouds
You can look down and see
How tiny everything is on earth.

So it is with our problems,
When we look at them close,
They seem so big.
When we view them from on high
They become small.

So the higher we go,
The smaller they are.
With your eye on the sparrow,
They eventually disappear.

I HAVE FOUND YOU

I heard your voice in the wind....
And I forgot the cold.
I saw your smile in the sun....And I was warm.
In the midst of a stormy sea, I spoke to you..
Touching a child's hand, I felt you so near
On an inky night filled with stars,
When it seemed the world stood still
And the silence was louder than thunder
I heard you answer.....
I know now,
That is where I shall meet you always...
In the silence....

ENLIGHTENMENT

I sat in my meditation garden
Waiting for you…
I sat silently letting troublesome thoughts
Pass me by……like wisps of wind…
I felt myself drifting towards a peaceful place
In that place,
Peace became my breath,
I felt the feeling of love…
My soul became calm
I became one with the sky, the trees and the wind.
Mystically, I touched the hem of the garment
And I was healed…
Returning, I finally knew,
I thought I was waiting for you…
When all along, you were waiting for me.

I HEARD YOU CALLING

I heard you calling me,
But I was too busy to answer.

I heard you calling,
Bu there were some things I had to do first.
I heard you calling,
But I was too tired to answer,

I heard you calling,
And I thought,
In just another minute I'll answer.

But you didn't call again,
And now,
I live my live
Listening.

LISTEN TO THE LITTLE VOICE

"Come with me" – child said.
"Let's run together towards Spring."
We'll be just like the butterfly that has just broken out of his cocoon.
We'll throw off our dark, winter clothes and dress in colors of
Yellow, pink, blue and royal purple.
We'll dance, sing and touch each flower.
We'll dip and spin and come to rest on a baby's chubby finger.
Everyone will see our beauty.
If we do these things, the world will follow our lead,
And we will soar high into the clouds going higher and higher..."

So, I did, and I see you did too!
And I turned to tell the child he was right,
But he was gone.
And I kept right on flying.

THE MIRROR OF INNER BEING

Have you ever really looked into someone's eyes?
They are the mirror of the person's inner being.
When you look into the eyes,
All aspects of the human form disappear...
It is in that moment that you connect spirit to spirit.
The mouth can smile,
The voice can lie,
The body can turn away from you,
But the eyes can only show you truth.
It is there that we are brothers.

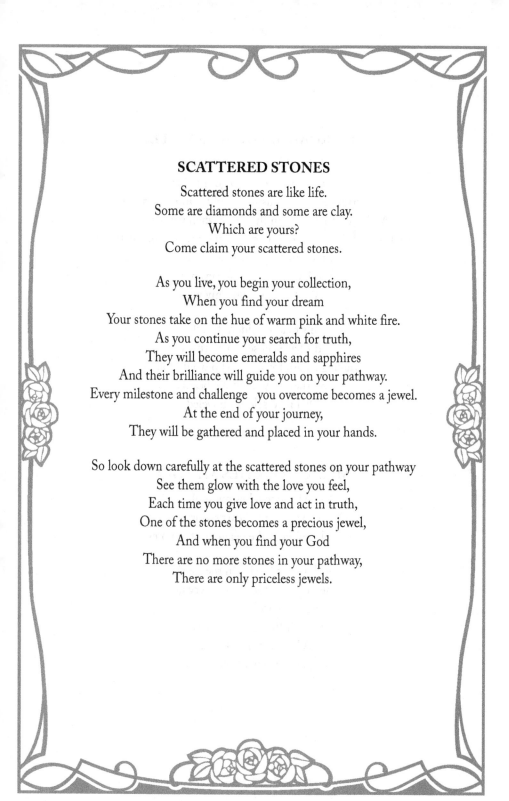

SCATTERED STONES

Scattered stones are like life.
Some are diamonds and some are clay.
Which are yours?
Come claim your scattered stones.

As you live, you begin your collection,
When you find your dream
Your stones take on the hue of warm pink and white fire.
As you continue your search for truth,
They will become emeralds and sapphires
And their brilliance will guide you on your pathway.
Every milestone and challenge   you overcome becomes a jewel.
At the end of your journey,
They will be gathered and placed in your hands.

So look down carefully at the scattered stones on your pathway
See them glow with the love you feel,
Each time you give love and act in truth,
One of the stones becomes a precious jewel,
And when you find your God
There are no more stones in your pathway,
There are only priceless jewels.

THE ROAD SELDOM TRAVELED

This road is seldom traveled,
But I have chosen to go this way.
My strides will raise dust on bright, sunny mornings
And leave footprints in the snow when winter comes.
As I walk, I delight in the fragrance and mystery of the forest,
I revel in warm summer breezes
And icy midnight, blue evenings,
As silver stars light my way.

This road is seldom traveled,
And I have chosen to go this way
Making a path for those who would follow
So they may share the beauty
Of a road seldom traveled.

MUSIC TOUCHES MY SOUL

Music touches my soul
As the door to my heart swings open
Welcoming in the beauty of the notes.

A Sense of God is in the music.
The Touch of God is in every note,
The Presence of God enfolds,
And I let this door of love open,
Where within the music
I am One with the One.

ONE WITH THE UNIVERSE

There is one heart, the heart of the universe,
we are all hearts beating in unison
With the one heart of the universe.
There is One Love, the Love of the Universe.
As we love, we love with the Heart of the Universe.
There is One Breath – The Breath of the Universe
We all breathe into this One Breath –
The Breath of the Universe.
There is One Life, the Life of the Universe.
We are all lives living in the One Life of the Universe.
The Universe is neither person, place nor thing..
The Universe is the One that live within us.
The One with whom our hearts beat in Unison with.
When we love, we love with the
Energy and Gentleness of the Universe.
When the heart gets tired, or sad, it, and finds itself alone. ,
The world around us gives no lasting comfort.
When the breath becomes shallow, labored and tight
And finds itself tired and lonely in the world.
It has drifted away from its' connection.
Life is like a symphony
When the conductor is prepared,
When all the Musical instruments are in tune,
And all the notes in their proper place,
The sound that is created is perfect.
We are the conductors, we are the musical instruments
We are the notes. when we are in tune with life,
We are the symphony, creating the music of a life well lived
with each other and with the heart of the Universe.

WHERE IS GOD?

How often I prayed to have a closer feeling of God.
To understand the mystery of all-embracing love.

And one morning I heard the beautiful sound of a guitar,
And I thought - that is God!
I listened to the laughter of little children
And I thought - that is God!

The scent of jasmine,
The feel of satin,
Beautiful sunrises and lavender sunsets,
A barren hill in Scotland
Grazing sheep in a meadow,
The beauty of free, wild horses,

All of this is God.
Expressions of the Presence
Here in our existence.

The search is over.
The prayer is answered.
God is! Everything!

THE PATH HOMEWARD

Walk with me,
We'll take the path that leads homeward.
We'll sit in the shade under the Bodi Tree
And listen to the song of the nightingale,
And drink in the scent of gardenias.
Gazing at the glorious blue sky,
And reaching our arms towards
The silken, billowing clouds
With hearts full of love,
We'll say,
Thank you God!

UNANSWERED QUESTIONS

Dancing sunbeams, tell me what music do you hear?
Blossoming begonias, tell me what is the secret of your beauty.
Green, moist grass, gently swaying in the June breezes,
Tell me what artist created your beautiful color.
Glorious Ocean, majestically powerful,
Tell me from what source you receive your strength and power.

Astounded at the beauty of the world around me,
I questioned and questioned,
But I received no response.
There was only Silence.

For a fleeting moment
I thought no one could answer the questions I posed,
Suddenly, the answers came
They were right there in the Silence.

For it is there, at the center of our being
That we meet with God,
Like a child returning from a long trip,
We drop our old baggage,
Run into the arms of our Creator
And all our questions are answered.
It is here, that we are one with our Source
As we live with and as our Creator.

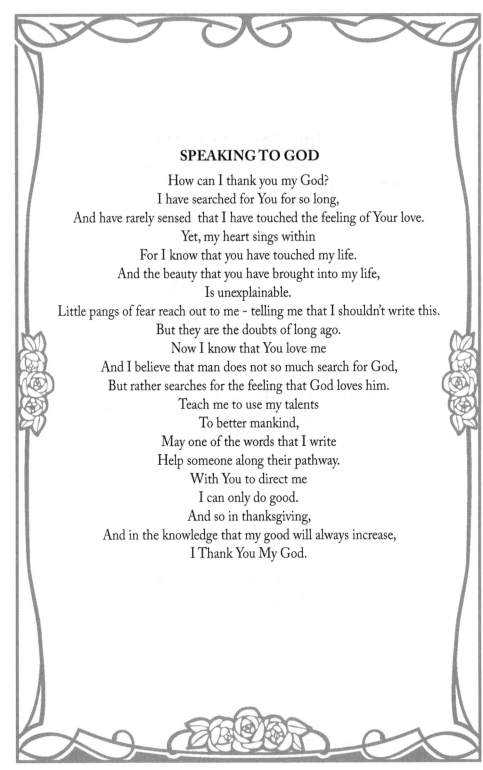

SPEAKING TO GOD

How can I thank you my God?
I have searched for You for so long,
And have rarely sensed that I have touched the feeling of Your love.
Yet, my heart sings within
For I know that you have touched my life.
And the beauty that you have brought into my life,
Is unexplainable.
Little pangs of fear reach out to me - telling me that I shouldn't write this.
But they are the doubts of long ago.
Now I know that You love me
And I believe that man does not so much search for God,
But rather searches for the feeling that God loves him.
Teach me to use my talents
To better mankind,
May one of the words that I write
Help someone along their pathway.
With You to direct me
I can only do good.
And so in thanksgiving,
And in the knowledge that my good will always increase,
I Thank You My God.

STANDING AT THE EDGE

What is it within us that keeps us standing at the edge?
We believe we are using caution.
We believe we are being careful.
We believe we are in control.

Standing at the edge is going through the motions of life.
It is that part of ego that prevents us from taking the first step to freedom.
It is that part of us that doesn't trust.
Standing at the edge – one can never feel the reviving tingle of the water.
Standing at the edge – one cannot experience the excitement of riding a wave.

Take the deep breath and plunge into the ocean of life.
Feel the spirit becoming alive within you.
Feel your spirit soaring, laughing, and resting, in the silence of the sea.

You are the ocean, the sun, and the stars.
You are me.
And I am you.
Stop standing at the edge,
For there is no edge when you are One with the One,
There is only joy in the silence.

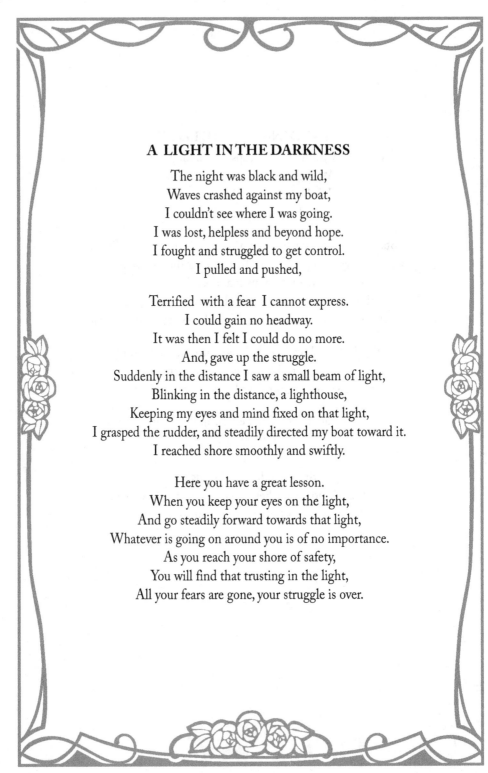

A LIGHT IN THE DARKNESS

The night was black and wild,
Waves crashed against my boat,
I couldn't see where I was going.
I was lost, helpless and beyond hope.
I fought and struggled to get control.
I pulled and pushed,

Terrified with a fear I cannot express.
I could gain no headway.
It was then I felt I could do no more.
And, gave up the struggle.
Suddenly in the distance I saw a small beam of light,
Blinking in the distance, a lighthouse,
Keeping my eyes and mind fixed on that light,
I grasped the rudder, and steadily directed my boat toward it.
I reached shore smoothly and swiftly.

Here you have a great lesson.
When you keep your eyes on the light,
And go steadily forward towards that light,
Whatever is going on around you is of no importance.
As you reach your shore of safety,
You will find that trusting in the light,
All your fears are gone, your struggle is over.

OUR SPECIAL SPACE

When we are born our Creator bestows us
With our own special space.
That precious space is ours alone.
And if by chance anyone
Steps into it, it jars our spirit
And shakes our being.
So dear one,
Respect my inheritance,
Touch not my special space
So my Spirit will remain Free
And
I will honor your special space too.

THE RIVER OF LIFE

The River of Life flows through each of us,
As the sun glistens and gleams
On the rivulets of the blue-green waters.
On the surface, all is smooth, calm and ever-moving.
However, beneath the water
Are the tempests that occur.
Rushing, pushing, rapids.
Secret whirlpools, treacherous rocks,
All the debris that we have carelessly tossed inside.

You are a river,
The sun shines on you,
Giving you life and movement.
Let the beautiful serenity that appears on the surface
Of the blue-green waters of your soul,
Exist above and beneath.
Then your life will flow in a clean, steady stream.

THEY TRIED TO CRUSH THE BEAUTIFUL FLOWER

They took a beautiful flower and tried to crush it.
They took a beautiful heart and tried to break it.
They took someone kind and good,
And because they didn't understand,
Tried to squelch it's spirit.
They took honor and pride, laughed at it, and chose deceit.
They took integrity and chose deception.

For a time it looked as if they might succeed.
But there is a higher Power, that created all the light in this Universe.
That light is eternal, and all powerful.
The lesson to be learned is that no one can darken Your Light.

Time has passed and they remain in their place of darkness.
Yet, the flower within is in full bloom,
The beautiful heart is full of love.
The Spirit is soaring higher than before,
Beauty, Integrity, Honor and Pride
Glisten like Gold on the surface of the face.

They, having tried to extinguish the light,
Shall stay forever in a place of darkness.
Huddled together,
Dark welcoming Dark,
For them, there will never be light.

Other Lands

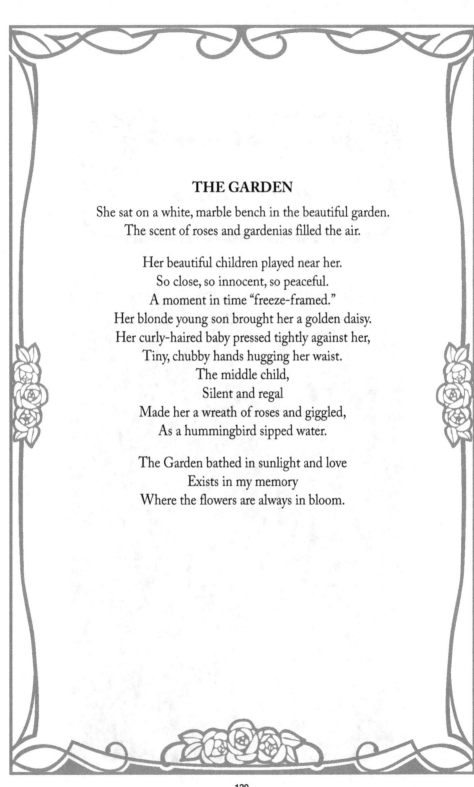

THE GARDEN

She sat on a white, marble bench in the beautiful garden.
The scent of roses and gardenias filled the air.

Her beautiful children played near her.
So close, so innocent, so peaceful.
A moment in time "freeze-framed."
Her blonde young son brought her a golden daisy.
Her curly-haired baby pressed tightly against her,
Tiny, chubby hands hugging her waist.
The middle child,
Silent and regal
Made her a wreath of roses and giggled,
As a hummingbird sipped water.

The Garden bathed in sunlight and love
Exists in my memory
Where the flowers are always in bloom.

MADRID
(Dedicated to Enrique)

Last night I traveled the road back to Madrid,
Standing on a high place,
I looked down at its sun bleached streets
Where I had silently walked so long ago,
And I whispered an "Ave."

As darkness fell
I heard once again the sound of castanets,
As we gathered round the campfire
Then the dancers clicked their heels
And burst on the scene, dazzling blurs of red and black,
Immersed in a beautiful, wild flamenco.

I drank the bitter wine, and sank my teeth hungrily into the sweet oranges.
Turning around, I saw the sand of the bullring drenched in blood,
And I shivered with delight to the echoes of the "OLE's."

The sun began to rise, the tambourines grew silent,
And the sound of castanets faded –
Somewhere a chapel bell tolled,
Calling all to prayer,
And once again I had to leave Madrid,
And as I did, I whispered an "Ave."

MEMORIES OF SEVILLE

Soft nights,
Inky skies with flashing stars,
The scent of oranges, tinged with jasmine.
Days bright with sun.
Every moment lived in tune to the sound of gypsy guitars.
It was my home
It is my soul,
And my longing for it never eases.
Sometimes I close my eyes and see a girl,
Carefree and young, full of the spirit of life
Dancing barefoot,
Swirling violet skirts, red satin sleeves.
A girl who left the sunny shores of Seville,
One day when the sky had darkened,
When love had ended.
Believing the sun would be shining on another shore.
But without one's soul, one cannot see the sun.
So I vow,
Someday, Someday I will return. Then the sun will shine again,
The guitars will sing again,
And I will dance barefoot again,
Reunited with my soul, ma Corazon.
And I will then live again!

MY SPAIN

My heart has longed for you, my Spain.
My heart longs with a pain and thirst
That cannot be quenched, my Spain.

To be at the seashore
To be in Barcelona
To walk again the streets of Madrid
To smell the orange blossoms
To hear the musical language,
To taste the wine…
How I long for you my Spain.

Someday, someday, I will return
Never to leave again, my Spain.

And I will let the sun kiss my face
And the sand warm my feet
And the cool marble of the piazza calm my heart.

I shall return to you,
I shall return to you
And I will no longer feel pain
For I will be home in your arms, my Spain.

MY SPANISH GRANDEE
(Dedicated to Enrique)

In mind I have lived in the Spain of old,
I have watched vaqueros ride golden Arabian stallions,
And sipped the sweet Andalusia wine.
I have knelt in prayer, my face covered by a heavy lace mantilla
And listened to the plaintive music of weeping, gypsy guitars,
That echoed the loss of my love.

The emptiness followed me into stately rooms and soaring Cathedrals.
Amidst the scent of luscious peaches, perfumed rose petals
and sandalwood incense.
How long it lasted.
Until I saw you again, "My Spanish Grandee!"
Bringing a touch of the Old World into my life,
Where memories of crystal chandeliers,
Burnished leather and golden sunrises
Once again become real!

I feel your hand in mine,
And I live again..
In Los Angeles – I found you!
Te Amo.

CI BON AY...

I heard the strains of the music
And I was transported
To another time, another place
Where I danced barefoot
Skirts swirling all around me
My hair flying to the notes of the gypsy guitar,
I felt alive again.

A gypsy whose heart belongs only to the music.
A child, a woman, a memory.
They called me Malayda
She lives imprinted on my soul like a brand
And when the music plays - her soul rejoices
And she dances,
And so do I.

THE DANCE OF LIFE

We clapped, we turned,
We changed partners in a sweet roundel
I soared; I flew, folded like a swan
En Pointe.
They clapped, they tapped,
They sang Gypsy words,
Skirts flowing
Boots clicking
Flamenco is alive!
Barely touching,
We glided around the floor,
Perfect movement, perfect form
Sailing together on the golden ballroom floor
Each person involved, each muscle tensed
The Mind dancing, the Soul in Bliss
All come together in the Dance of Life.

SING ME A SONG OF THE PAST

Sing me a song of the old times,
Let me feel once again, the peace of being a free spirit.
Sitting by the blue, Aegean Sea,
We laughed, we loved, and we danced,
For we had the music
The bread of our lives.

The past is never really past,
It lives in your veins, your heart, your soul...

Come with me, sit by the campfire,
In the shade of the Alhambra,
And let the music seep into your being
And free you,
Come and be born again,
Come in your Mind,
And find where you left your soul . . .

THE GYPSY

The woman sat silent and still
As dark as the unlit room.

As the wind gently rose
The beaded curtains swayed and jingled.
Then a beam of moonlight lit the room,
And I saw her, The Gypsy.

How many times have I dreamt of her?
What was she trying to tell me?
Hair black and wild,
Eyes deep filled with fire,
Skin creamy and warm as honey,
Hands reaching out towards me.
Like a phantom she was dressed in swirls of silk
Red, blue, green, orange and gold.
Without words she told me she was waiting for me.
She had been longing to see me.

She beckoned to me and I ran into her arms.
I was home and felt alive again,
Vowing never again to deny my real self,
I took my place,
And I sat silent and still,
As dark as the unlit room.

FAREWELL TO ENGLAND

Last night I dreamt that I was once again
At Charring Cross, hiding from the King.
So much has happened in my life
Since the day I first met him.
And, although my heart tells me to go to him,
My head dictates otherwise.

What is waiting for me beyond that corner?
If I could believe in the glory of love
I would gladly have myself found.
But men surround him, and twist and muddle
The mind and kind heart he possesses.

And so I flee - towards the White Cliffs of Dover,
Across the Channel to France..
Leaving behind my heart and my country.
When all is said and done, what is it that moves one?
The leanings of the heart or the rulings of the head.
I leave my heart and follow my head.
So farewell England, farewell my Sovereign,
Farewell moors and heather,

Farewell dancing round the Maypole.
Farewell.
In another time, in another life
I shall return
And find the love I had to leave.

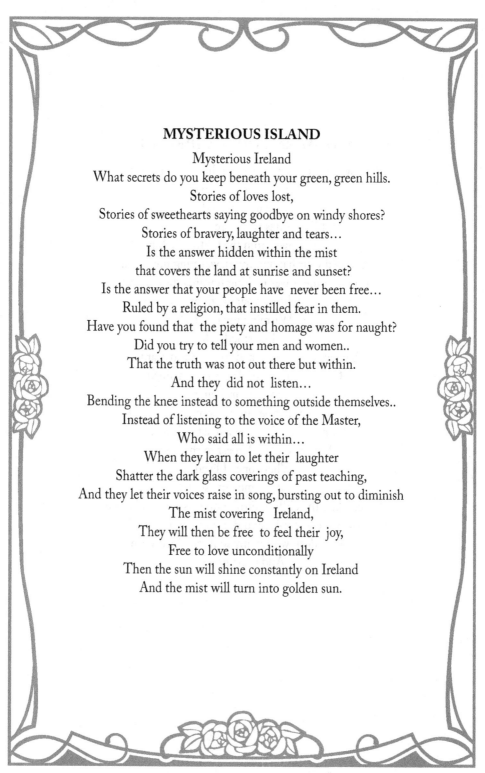

MYSTERIOUS ISLAND

Mysterious Ireland
What secrets do you keep beneath your green, green hills.
Stories of loves lost,
Stories of sweethearts saying goodbye on windy shores?
Stories of bravery, laughter and tears...
Is the answer hidden within the mist
that covers the land at sunrise and sunset?
Is the answer that your people have never been free...
Ruled by a religion, that instilled fear in them.
Have you found that the piety and homage was for naught?
Did you try to tell your men and women..
That the truth was not out there but within.
And they did not listen...
Bending the knee instead to something outside themselves..
Instead of listening to the voice of the Master,
Who said all is within...
When they learn to let their laughter
Shatter the dark glass coverings of past teaching,
And they let their voices raise in song, bursting out to diminish
The mist covering Ireland,
They will then be free to feel their joy,
Free to love unconditionally
Then the sun will shine constantly on Ireland
And the mist will turn into golden sun.

THE WARM SOUL OF IRELAND

Wind swept isle, misty sea, green hills, watery peat bogs,
Memories of days past,
Rise in my mind,
Like sprites rising from the sea.
Gazing down from the Cliffs of Mohr
I sensed your hand in mind, warming my soul...
In the roar of the waves rushing towards the craggy coast,
I heard your laughter,
Warming my heart
Time stood still
And every care, tear, and worry was discarded.
Only memories of days past remained,
Warming my being.
In that beautiful moment,
I raised my heart in a toast to love...
A toast to life...A toast to the past...
Where once I lived.
And it warmed my soul....
Descending the cliffs, returning to this time and place,
I felt the wind and rain, and the cold numbed my hands,
Though deep within, my soul remained warm.
And remains so.

THE MISTS OF GERMANY"S FORESTS

I watched the mist rise from the forest,
It curled, twisted and changed color
From gray to black to wispy white.
Rising, thin and light
Yet - strong and persistent.

Stately oaks and pines disappeared as
The mist rose and connected with the sky,
In a mystical slow-moving dance.

And I thought
How like man is the forest
We are the oak, the pine and maple.
The mist is thin, fine with no definite form
You cannot touch it, contain or climb it.
Yet, its strength is such
That it can cause entire forests to disappear.
If we are the trees,
Then the mist is what we pull over ourselves
To hide, to run away, to deny our destiny.

We must fear not,
For the mists are only illusions
Created to hide behind,
We must boldly stand forward
Take our place in the order of life,
Letting nothing deter us,
Nor obscure our strength and beauty.
Piercing the mist, we must take our place in the sun.

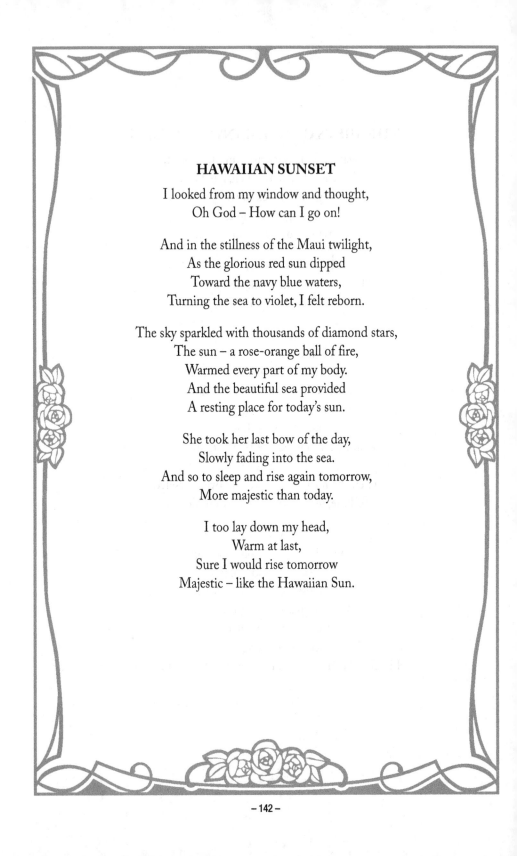

HAWAIIAN SUNSET

I looked from my window and thought,
Oh God – How can I go on!

And in the stillness of the Maui twilight,
As the glorious red sun dipped
Toward the navy blue waters,
Turning the sea to violet, I felt reborn.

The sky sparkled with thousands of diamond stars,
The sun – a rose-orange ball of fire,
Warmed every part of my body.
And the beautiful sea provided
A resting place for today's sun.

She took her last bow of the day,
Slowly fading into the sea.
And so to sleep and rise again tomorrow,
More majestic than today.

I too lay down my head,
Warm at last,
Sure I would rise tomorrow
Majestic – like the Hawaiian Sun.

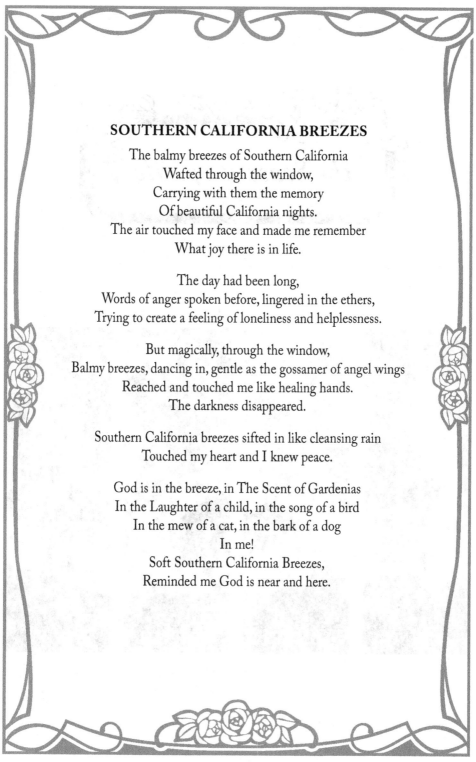

SOUTHERN CALIFORNIA BREEZES

The balmy breezes of Southern California
Wafted through the window,
Carrying with them the memory
Of beautiful California nights.
The air touched my face and made me remember
What joy there is in life.

The day had been long,
Words of anger spoken before, lingered in the ethers,
Trying to create a feeling of loneliness and helplessness.

But magically, through the window,
Balmy breezes, dancing in, gentle as the gossamer of angel wings
Reached and touched me like healing hands.
The darkness disappeared.

Southern California breezes sifted in like cleansing rain
Touched my heart and I knew peace.

God is in the breeze, in The Scent of Gardenias
In the Laughter of a child, in the song of a bird
In the mew of a cat, in the bark of a dog
In me!
Soft Southern California Breezes,
Reminded me God is near and here.

The Seasons of Life

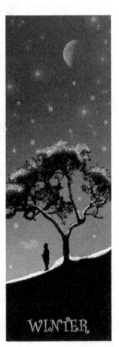

SPRING SUMMER AUTUMN WINTER

HAPPY NEW YEAR

When we think of New Year's Eve, we think of
Horns blowing, music playing,
Elegantly dressed, perfumed ladies and tuxedo-clad men.
Resolutions to be made, and parties to attend,
Rushing to get out of the house on time.
But wait – there is something that came for you - marked,
"DO NOT OPEN UNTIL JANUARY 1ST."

Every year you receive this package.
Each year in your rush, you leave it unopened.
The box is beautifully wrapped and filled with
The gifts of health, harmony,
Prosperity, love, and creativity.

They are your gifts.
You have always had these gifts,
But you have not taken the time to accept them
Or, maybe began to open the package and stopped half-way.

This year, unwrap the box, untie the ribbon, unseal the box,
Accept the gifts, all are yours to have,
There is only one thing you have to do,
Accept the blessings and talents given to you.
Happy New Year!
Let this year be the beginning of all the
Wonderful New Year's of your life.

MARCH WINDS...A RENEWAL

I watched the March winds play with the leaves.
Tossing and blowing them to and fro.
Performing a Merry Dance.
They leaped, pirouetted, rose and fell to earth with no direction.
The wind put them through their paces, not caring what their name or origin.
With great force it performed a movement of energy without direction.
So it is with our Lives.

We are like the Wind.
Putting our thoughts through their paces, raising them up, tossing them around
And causing them to fall to earth with a Thud.
Or,
We can, like the Wind,
When calm and warm, directs the leaves to earth,
Allowing them to nestle in the ground,
To enrich the soil for the spring planting, and new life.
We must,
Calm our minds,
Direct our thoughts to rise upwards,
To the peaceful warmth of the sun.
In this way we will enrich our lives,
As we nurture our minds and prepare it for renewal
Filling the earth with the wonders of all our good thoughts
It is then we can reap the harvest of all we have planted.

A CELEBRATION OF SPRING

Can you smell the fresh, wet earth?
Gently bathed by today's spring shower.
Isn't it beautiful?

Can you see the bright, blue sky?
With a hint of a rainbow,
Dazzling your mind with its beauty?
Isn't it beautiful?

Can you see the tulip bulb pushing it's
Pretty, perky yellow head through the ground?
Isn't it beautiful?

Do you know all these things have been
put here by God
Who loves you.
Isn't it beautiful?

Do you know that God loves, and lives
In You as You?
Isn't it beautiful?

THOUGHTS IN JUNE

As I sat here thinking of June,
So many things came to mind.
Thoughts of Graduation Days.
As graduates step forward toward their future.
Thoughts of Wedding Days,
As young couples pledge their love
and commit their lives to each other.
Thoughts of Father's Day,
And the feeling of love and appreciation
For all those men who have done their best to
Love and care for their children.
So, for these things, I thought I would take the
Newly bloomed June Roses I have gathered
And lovingly give them all to the
Fathers, Mothers, Graduates, Brides and Grooms.
And, of course, this special one for you.

SWEET SEPTEMBER

Sweet September you kiss my cheek with your golden sun.
The warm breezes of this month of harvest
Touch me and seep deep into my being.
I see, and feel and live again in the glory of September
And know that the Harvest time is now.
This abundance, this golden sun
Surrounds and envelopes me
And as I lift my head upwards
Towards the sun and God, my Source,
I know I live and move and have my being in an unending harvest.
For this, I am grateful.

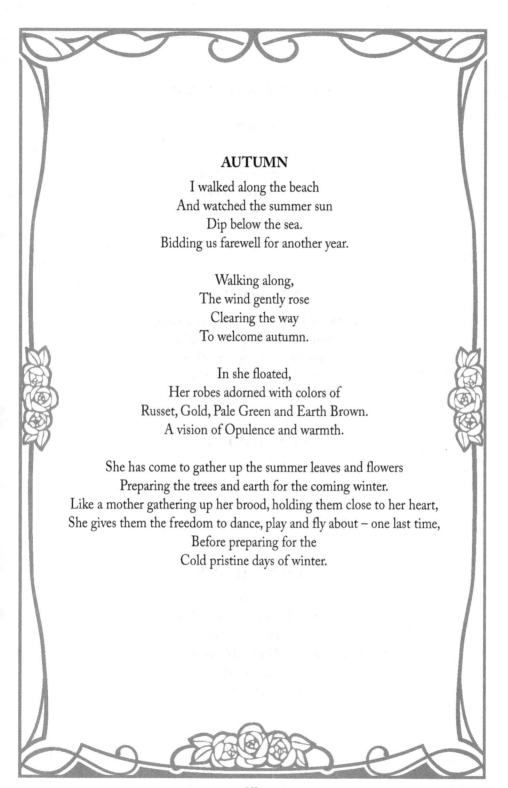

AUTUMN

I walked along the beach
And watched the summer sun
Dip below the sea.
Bidding us farewell for another year.

Walking along,
The wind gently rose
Clearing the way
To welcome autumn.

In she floated,
Her robes adorned with colors of
Russet, Gold, Pale Green and Earth Brown.
A vision of Opulence and warmth.

She has come to gather up the summer leaves and flowers
Preparing the trees and earth for the coming winter.
Like a mother gathering up her brood, holding them close to her heart,
She gives them the freedom to dance, play and fly about – one last time,
Before preparing for the
Cold pristine days of winter.

THOUGHTS IN SEPTEMBER

ONCE

Once you held me.
Once you listened to me
Once you loved me.
Then you left me.
I still love you.
For this, I am grateful.

MY PROMISE

I promised myself one day I would laugh
Sure I could keep that promise,
You broke all your promises,
Now, I have broken mine,
I can't laugh.

COMMITMENT

Not ready for commitment you say,
Sounds like a life term in an insane asylum?
You're only supposed to love someone,
Not commit them - or to them.

A SPECIAL KISS

Yesterday a bunny kissed me.
I laughed and cried with delight.
It may seem such a little thing,
But to be kissed by God's innocent being
Reminded me,
This is what love really is.

BEAUTIFUL DECEMBER

The month of frosted windowpanes,
Thoughts of loved ones.
Crackling fires,
Cookies baking,
Homes filled with Love, laughter
And the wonder of children
A time of family and expectation.

December is Christmas.
The glow of Christmas lights,
The smell of pine
Days wrapped in bright ribbons
Nights wrapped in the warmth of Love.
December is beautiful memories.

CHRISTMAS SHOPPING

As I walked on the hard packed snow,
Thinking of what I would get you for Christmas,
I saw glowing in a window –
A beautiful candle.
Its flame wavered, and danced, casting a myriad of beautiful colors
Where I stood on the cold, white snow.
As I gazed at the candle,
I thought how beautiful are the simple things of nature,
And I knew what to give you.
I shall give you light when your world is darkest.
Warmth, when the day has been cold
And the cold has reached down to your very bones.
Bright, beautiful colors of the rainbow
To dress up your world,
A haven to come to when you are lonely,
And a light that never goes out,
Always burning brightly, welcoming you home.
Merry Christmas

Maria's poems are filled with passion and truth. You will weep, sigh and laugh out loud. Her words are equivalent to touching your Soul. Everyone should have this experience. Maria, you have put into words all our life experiences and have begun your life's work. Congratulations.

Life long friend, Paula Swornay
International Opera Singer,
Actress, Ms. Senior California 2003

Be prepared to laugh, to cry, to remember the good times and the not so good times, all that life brings. But most of all, be prepared to be touched by Maria Hughes' humor, wit and exceptionally loving and open heart. You'll want to read it over and over again!"

Kathleen Caputo
Minister of Religious Science

I am honored to write an endorsement. "Rev. Maria Hughes has an open mind compassionate heart and a desire to enrich the lives of all she meets, prepare yourself to be inspired, uplifted, and positively changed by her marvelous words."

Rev. Karen Gigante
Interior Decorator and a
grateful student of Maria Hughes